CONTEST CHARTS

Doris Chase Doane

First printing 1986
ISBN Number: 0-86690-315-1
Library of Congress Catalog Card Number: 85-73314

Cover Design: Lynda Kay Fullerton

Published by:
American Federation of Astrologers, Inc.
P.O. Box 22040, 6534 South Rural Road
Tempe, Arizona 85282

Printed in the United States of America

BOOKS BY DORIS CHASE DOANE

HOROSCOPES OF THE U.S. PRESIDENTS

ASTROLOGY: 30 YEARS RESEARCH

INDEX TO THE BROTHERHOOD OF LIGHT LESSONS

TIME CHANGES IN U.S.A.

TAROT CARD SPREAD READER (with King Keyes)

ZODIAC: KEY TO CAREER (with C. Peel)

TIME CHANGES IN CANADA AND MEXICO

TIME CHANGES IN THE WORLD

ASTROLOGY RULERSHIPS

HOW TO PREPARE AND PASS AN ASTROLOGY CERTIFICATE EXAM

HOW TO READ COSMODYNES

PROGRESSIONS IN ACTION

VOCATIONAL SELECTION AND COUNSELING, Vol. I and II

ASTROLOGY AS A BUSINESS

ACCURATE WORLD HOROSCOPES

ASTROLOGERS QUESTION BOX

DOANE'S 1981-1985 WORLD WIDE TIME CHANGE UPDATE

CONTEST CHARTS

CONTENTS

Mind is the Master Power that moulds and makes And Man is Mind, and evermore he takes The tool of thought, and shaping what he wills, Brings forth a thousand joys, a thousand ills; He thinks in secret and it comes to pass: Environment is his looking glass.

-- **James Allen**

1. FUNDAMENTAL APPROACH

Amazing results come from applying a simple set of rules to judge winners of various kinds of contests. That branch of astrology called horary astrology not only gives us the rules, but by using them a person can prove or disprove astrology for himself in a short period of time.

Success with horary astrology depends upon two important factors: Asking the question at the proper time, and wording the question precisely. A confused question (often containing more than one idea instead of a single, sharp-pointed thought) will invariably result in a confused chart, which will be difficult if not impossible to read.

A horary chart is really the portrayal of a mental event. And research has proven that a chart for a mental event can be judged much the same as a natal chart. While the mind is forming the question - new factors are being added to the original thought that change the trend - a mental event is under gestation.

This process is comparable to a fetus undergoing a period of gestation. After the question becomes crystal clear and the desire to know the answer is strong, it manifests externally from the subconscious mind, moving from the mental to the physical world as a child at birth moves into the external world from the womb of its mother. From an astrological point of view, then, the birth of a question or an idea is the moment when it is expressed verbally or in writing.

A word of caution - sometimes in our haste to get on with it, we ask improper questions. The question should always be examined to see if the two basic requirements mentioned above are fulfilled. Is this the proper time to ask the question? Is there a strong feeling to know the answer?

Is my question worded properly, asking exactly what I want to know? If the question has been asked properly, and the urge to know the answer is deep-seated and strong, there will be no difficulty in determining which houses to look to in the chart that represent the activities surrounding that which has been asked about.

TIMING THE QUESTION

To know "Is this the proper time to ask the question?" several conditions dealing with environment should be examined. For instance, a querent would not stand much chance of success constructing outdoor swimming pools in northern Alaska, or starting a business selling ski equipment in the Sahara. Why? Because the environment is not conducive to the sort of success, and there is no need by the customers in those areas.

Just as in horary charts, in contest charts environment is also an important factor - both the inner and outer environment. Inner environment is the subconscious mind where the mental event takes place. Further, that inner environment is fortified when the outer environment is defined and slanted toward the questioned situation. Then conditions will be appropriate to answer the question.

For instance, the proper time (environment) for asking about political contests is after the candidates have been nominated. The same timing element holds true when judging which side in a game of sport will win - after the contestants have been named.

Similarly, when applying the horary technique to determine the sex of an unborn child, it would be wise to wait to ask the question after it has been learned that the prospective mother is pregnant, for example.

It bears restating: This environment issue is also most important in judging contest charts. There is no doubt but that clearer answers result with more ease from considering circumstances surrounding the condition asked about by waiting until the questioned situation has had time to form and jell in the subconscious mind or level of awareness. Then, to energize the question, a deep desire to know the outcome forms and presents the proper time to ask the question.

WORDING THE QUESTION

Anyone, whether he is a contestant or not, can ask a question about a contest. Nevertheless, certain conditions will determine how the chart should be considered and interpreted.

Contest charts are divided in two by mentally drawing a vertical line down through the horoscope from top to bottom. The east side of the chart represents the challenger or one asked about, and the west side maps the opposition. The seventh house becomes the first house of the opponent and the fourth house becomes the tenth house of honor for the opposition.

If a person asks about himself as one of the contestants, he is signified by the eastern side of the wheel. This type of chart is demonstrated in Chapter Five, *One Against the Field*. However, when a question involves two contending parties, the chart division shows the first party to be ruled by the east side and the opposing party, by the west side.

Sometimes there is no definite challenger and defender. In such cases, careful wording of the question is required to arrive at an answer. The chief interest of the person asking the question puts the team he thinks of first on the east side. In other cases, the first party mentioned would be mapped by the eastern side.

When only one side is mentioned (like in "Will the Red Sox win the World Series?") the team mentioned is allotted to the east. Even though unspoken, the implied opposition is ruled by the west side of the wheel.

CONTEST CHART DATA

In addition to the horary approach to reading contest charts, there is the electional chart which can be used to determine the outcome of a contest. This chart is cast for the moment a contest starts. Here, because he takes the initiative, the challenger is represented by the east side of the horoscope, and his opponent by the west side. When there is a champion, it is customary for him not to issue a challenge, but to accept or reject any proposed to him. Regardless of who is champion, the person who issues the challenge is represented by the east side of the chart, and the one who receives the challenge, by the west side.

After the three basic requirements are fulfilled, i.e., the environment has been considered, the desire to know is strong, and the question is worded properly, the horary contest chart is erected for the date, place and moment when these factors become clear and distinct. Then, and only then, can the delineation factors reflect the outcome of a contest.

1-2-3 JUDGMENT

A contest properly belongs to the tenth house of a chart because the tenth house maps victory, honor, credit and power. In winning a game, a prize fight, or an election, the main object is the honor to be gained, although money or other considerations may be of secondary importance. Therefore, the probable success of a contestant or a team is judged by the strength and harmony of the house of honor, the tenth.

Of an almost equal importance is the first house, which pictures the luck, ability, skill and technique (personal prowess) of the contestant. Particular attention, then, should be paid to the first and tenth houses where the contestant or team asked about is concerned. When judging the ability and honor of the opposition, that same attention should be directed to the seventh and fourth houses (which are the first and tenth houses of the opposition).

Let us go back to the horary chart. The person asking the question (the querent) is denoted by the first house. In those horary charts set for personal questions, the Moon (everyday affairs) is considered to be co-ruler of the first house, regardless which zodiacal sign appears on the ascendant.

However, in these contest charts we are dealing with two contenders. The person asking about the outcome of the contest between the two steps to one side, and the Moon is no longer his co-ruler. In fact, in contest charts the person asking the question is not given a place in the horoscope, not unless he is a contestant as explained in Chapter Five.

After judging the first and tenth houses, the following factors should be taken into consideration. The planets, except Mars and Saturn, on the east side of the chart favor the first party, especially if placed in the first or tenth house. But if planets appear on the west side of the chart, especially in the seventh and fourth (opponent's ability and honor respectfully), they favor the opposition. Should these planets be afflicted they lessen the odds for winning. The luck factor is mapped by planets, and those that are malefic, either by nature or by aspect) detract from the ability to win.

As in natal astrology, the ability to master the personality or not is also significant. If the ruler of the first house appears in the first or tenth house, there is an indication that the first party is the master of his own personality and power. But should that ruler of the first house be located in the seventh house or fourth house, then the opponent exercises an authority over the first party. Conversely, if the opponent's ruler is in the tenth or first house, then the challenger has authority over the opponent. More power and luck are indicated when the planets appear on the same side of the chart that they rule. Usually the more powerful and harmonious half of the chart denotes the winner.

That's the 1-2-3 of picking a winner with horary: (1) the honor (tenth house) of each side, (2) the luck and ability (first house) of each side, and (3) planetary distribution - number, malefics and benefics on each side.

Before demonstrating these steps in delineating actual example charts, there is one other thought to be clarified. Outdoor contests, such as races involving cars, dogs, horses, marathoners, etc., not to mention games like baseball, football, tennis, soccer, etc., are affected by the weather.

In the strict sense of contest parlance, the weather may be a hazard. Therefore, weather is allotted to the fifth house of the chart (hazards) in this connotation, even though the weather per se is governed by the fourth house in a horoscope.

GUIDELINES

For ease in learning the most from reading the example charts in this book, you should copy the chart onto a horoscope blank so that you can see plainly how the 1-2-3 of judging contests is accomplished. Or, if you have a computer and printer, you can punch in the data in order to have the astrological pattern in front of you as you read the text in this book.

These interpretations are based upon three double-rulership signs: Scorpio ruled by Pluto and Mars; Aquarius ruled by Uranus and Saturn; and Pisces ruled by Neptune and Jupiter in the tropical zodiac. Geocentric positions of the planets are given, and the house cusps are calculated according to the placidian system.

Aspects are based upon the following orbs which take into consideration the strength of a house that a planet occupies as well as the distance from the perfect aspect (see Figure).

ASPECTS AND THEIR ORBS*

ASPECT	DEG	SYM	CADENT		SUCCEDENT		ANGULAR		SYM	DEG	ASPECT
			P	L	P	L	P	L			
SEMISEXTILE	30	⊻	1°	2°	2°	3°	3°	4°	⊼	150	INCONJUNCT
SEMISQUARE	45	∠	3	4	4	5	5	6	⬚	135	SESQUISQUARE
SEXTILE	60	*	5	6	6	7	7	8	*	60	SEXTILE
SQUARE	90	□	6	8	8	10	10	12	△	120	TRINE
OPPOSITION	180	☌	8	11	10	13	12	15	♂	0	CONJUNCTION

DEG = degrees
SYM = symbol
P = Planets
L = Luminaries (Sun and Moon)

M.C. and Asc. have the same orb as planets in angles.
Orb of the Parallel aspect is always one degree.
NATAL: Always use the larger orb.
PROGRESSED: Effective orb of all major, minor, or transit progressed aspects is always one degree.

Aspects on all charts in this book were calculated according to this table.

*From *How to Read Cosmodynes*[6]

After copying the chart, assign contestant rulership, to the east and west side of the chart, then apply the 1-2-3 factors:

(1) Look to each side's tenth and first houses to determine honor (tenth) and ability, skill and technique (first).

(2) Check each side's luck factor: Benefics (Jupiter and Venus), malefic planets (Saturn and Mars), aspects (strength), and planetary positions.

Following this approach allows us to build the basics and then work on them to decide the outcomes of the contest.

2. PRIZE FIGHTS

Some of the most enthusiastic sports fans are those who are devoted watchers of boxing matches. They can usually tell you who the champion was in any given year, and recite the statistics of each and every bout. But there exists a challenging and exciting way for these fans to get a bigger bang out of their hobby. Contest charts can afford them foresight on the outcome.

At the championship level there are twelve classes offering plentiful opportunities to apply this technique. These include heavyweight, light heavyweight, middleweight, junior middleweight, welterweight, junior welterweight, light weight, junior lightweight, featherweight, junior featherweight, bantamweight and flyweight.

Aside from these professional matches there are many other bouts that provide challenges to test contest charts. Whether the fight is on a professional or amateur level, fans usually pick a favorite contestant, especially now that so many sporting events are no farther away than the nearest television set.

After a fight is advertised, the question can be posed as to who will win. First, there is a puzzling over whether the favorite will come out on top. As time goes on the media provides opinions before the fight starts. This stimulates an urgency to ask the question. The chart is cast for that moment as discussed in Chapter One.

ROBINSON VS. FULLMER

Back in 1960 I was still testing the contest technique. The day before this fight I asked, "Will Sugar Ray Robinson take Gene Fullmer tomorrow night?" That question was asked at 8:30 A.M. Pacific Standard Time, on December 2, 1960, at 34N04 118W15. The contest chart was erected for that data .

Cusps: MC 22 ♎ 27, 11th 19 ♍ 07, 12th 11 ♐ 38, ASC 3 ♑ 26, 2nd 9 ♒ 05, and 3rd 18 ♓ 52.

Planetary positions:

Zodiac	Declinations	Zodiac	Declinations
☉ 10 ♐ 30	22S01	♄ 16 ♑ 19	22S17
☽ 04 ♊ 54	16N10	♅ 25 ♌ 48Rx	13N37
☿ 23 ♍ 45	16S52	♆ 10 ♍ 00	13S11
♀ 20 ♑ 52	24S02	♀ 08 ♍ 08	20N15
♂ 17 ♋ 39Rx	24N50	MC 22 ♎ 27	08S44
♃ 07 ♑ 26	23S16	ASC 03 ♑ 26	23S24

As Robinson's name was the first one mentioned, he is indicated by the east side of the chart. His prowess (first house) is described by the position and aspects of the Ascendant, Jupiter, Saturn and Venus (planets in the house).

Robinson's honor (tenth house) is signified by the aspects of the Midheaven, Neptune in the tenth house, and Venus because it rules the sign of Libra on the house cusp. Venus is located in his first house which seems to indicate that he will have control over his honor.

All of the mentioned planets appear in angular houses - the strongest houses in the chart. That plus the fact that Robinson has more planets on his side of the chart than Fullmer does depicts strength. Remember that nothing is accomplished without energy (aspects, strength) in a chart.

Fullmer's honor (the fourth house in this chart) is ruled by Mars because Aries appears on this house cusp. Mars is located in his first house (the seventh here), again mapping the fact that he may also have control over his own honor. Mars is opposition Saturn and Venus signifying that Fullmer would have tough competition.

Ruling Cancer on Fullmer's first house, the Moon patterns a T-square with Pluto and the Sun. Overall, these configurations do not portray much luck even though Fullmer was champion at the time.

Going back to Robinson's side we note that Venus is square the Midheaven. A square symbolizes an obstacle to be surmounted. In addition to that influence, a T-square involving Mars, the conjunction of Saturn-Venus and the

Midheaven pictures stress for both contestants, because this T-square involves positions on each side of the chart.

No matter where Neptune falls in these charts, or even how it is aspected (supportive or restrictive), the conditions its maps are always clouded and indistinct. Due to this nebulous situation, judgment of the department it rules is sometimes difficult to interpret.

Even though Neptune in this house of Robinson's honor (tenth) receives a sextile from Jupiter in the first house, circumstances surrounding the bout were anything but definitive. A Neptune-Jupiter aspect often coincides with a certain amount of overconfidence, or the euphoric state of expecting more than reality can produce.

A malefic planet is deposited in each contestant's first house; Robinson with Saturn, and Fullmer, Mars. Both benefics, Jupiter and Venus, appear in Robinson's favor - also in his first house.

Balancing all of these factors, we would think that Robinson had a narrow edge to win the bout. However, this chart is really too closely balanced to call a win or make any statement as to the outcome of the contest.

In the end, the judges called the bout a draw. When the announcement was made from center ring, the crowd rose to its feet and booed for ten minutes. They felt strongly that Sugar Ray should have won. Ah, Neptune, that precursor of confusion!

MACHIN vs MAXIM

Next we look at a chart for the bout between Eddie Machin and Joe Maxim. Before this, Machin had had 20 wins in 20 bouts. He was 20 years old at the time. Would this be number 21 for him?

"Will Eddie Machin win?" was the question. The chart is set for May 3, 1957, 34N04 118W15, at 6:30 P.M. Pacific Daylight Time, a couple of hours before the fight took place .

Cusps: MC 3 ♌ 47, 11th 6 ♍ 26, 12th 5 ♎ 34, ASC 00 ♏ 15, 2nd 28 ♏ 53, and 3rd 00 ♑ 23.

Planetary positions:

Zodiac	Declination	Zodiac	Declination
☉ 13 ♉ 20	15N49	♄ 13 ♐ 00Rx	20S30
☽ 03 ♋ 41	19N39	♅ 03 ♌ 06	20N03
☿ 16 ♉ 25	17N34	♆ 00 ♍ 53Rx	10S05
♀ 18 ♉ 26	16N48	♇ 27 ♌ 56	22N44
♂ 29 ♊ 39	24N44	MC 03 ♌ 47	19N17
♃ 23 ♍ 10Rx	04N29	ASC 00 ♏ 15	20S17

This is a confusing chart for several reasons. In the first place asking the question at a more appropriate time might have resulted in a clearer chart, one more easily judged. Yes, there is Neptune again!

In horary charts when we see less than three degrees or more than twenty-eight degrees rising on the ascendant, we call the chart "not radical" - usually meaning unreadable. In contest charts this has not been definitely proven or disproven. In any case, caution should be used in the delineation of such charts. Here we have an Ascendant of less than three degrees rising, so the question may have come up prematurely.

As Machin's name was mentioned first, he is represented by the east side (left) of the chart. His honor (tenth house) is mapped by the activity of the Midheaven, Pluto in the house, and the Sun ruling Leo on the cusp of the house. Note that the Sun is located on Maxim's side.

Machin's prowess is pictured by the Ascendant, Neptune in the first house, and Pluto and Mars as co-rulers of his Scorpio Ascendant. Pluto appears in his own tenth house, but Mars falls on Maxim's side.

Maxim's technique and ability, mapped by the seventh house, his first in this chart, are signified by the Sun, Mercury and Venus, none of which are involved in many strong aspects. Therefore, they do not represent a great deal of power.

Maxim's honor, mapped by the fourth house in this chart (but considered as his tenth) holds no planets, showing no action and a weakness. Because the double rulership sign of Aquarius occupies the house cusp, Uranus and Saturn become co-rulers. They are split between sides:

Saturn on the east (Machin), and Uranus on the west (Maxim).

The planets malefic in nature are divided: Saturn on Machin's side, and Mars on Maxim's side. The same situation describes the chart positions of the benefic planets: Jupiter on Machin's side and Venus on Maxim's. Neither side seems to clearly outweigh the other. Because there is more power on Maxim's side, we might give him the edge. However, everything about this chart is iffy - especially the position of Neptune in Machin's first house. Also, note that no planets appear in Maxim's tenth house.

Outcome: This was a 10-round heavyweight match, during which there were no knockouts (a first for Machin). When the judges' decision was announced, it was unanimously in favor of Machin. Here again Neptune seemed to foreshadow what the outcome actually would be.

The first horoscopes presented in this book are given to show some of the foibles of reading contest charts, not to belabor the fact that Neptune is nebulous or that maps "not radical" cannot be read - just that caution is needed in delineating them.

ARAGON vs BASILIO

Here is another case of less than three degrees rising. However, in this instance the chart itself is a clear-cut indication of a winner without applying time consuming analysis.

At the time there was a great deal of speculation about this fight, which took place in September 1958. The question was, "Will Art Aragon defeat Carmen Basilio?" The chart was set for August 21, 1958, 34N04 118W15, at 10:20 A.M. Pacific Daylight Time.

Cusps: MC 20 ♑ 07, 11th 15 ♒ 34, 12th 18 ♓ 53, ASC 02 ♉ 30, 2nd 03 ♊ 45, and 3rd, 27 ♊ 39.

Planetary positions:

Zodiac	Declination	Zodiac	Declination
☉ 28 ♌ 37	12N09	♄ 19 ♐ 06sta	21S45
☽ 03 ♐ 39	16N49	♅ 13 ♌ 03	17N32
☿ 01 ♍ 18Rx	06N28	♆ 02 ♏ 25	10S41
♀ 07 ♌ 32	19N05	♀ 01 ♍ 54	21N24
♂ 18 ♉ 17	14N57	MC 20 ♑ 07	21S47
♃ 27 ♎ 17	09S27	ASC 02 ♉ 30	12N22

Dividing the chart, we allot Aragon's honor and ability to the east side, and Basilio's to the west side. Even though Neptune falls in the seventh house of the opposition, a brief glance at the chart reveals that all of the planets except Mars in the first house appear on Basilio's side. That is power and luck!

With a chart such as this there is little or no need to do anything at all to judge the outcome. Certainly not the procedural 1-2-3. The chart clearly indicates it. Aragon was defeated by a technical knockout in the eighth round.

Just as all rules are made to be broken, this is a prime example that the "less than 3 degrees or more than 28 degrees" maxim is not infallible. In some rare cases, the chart is so one-sided as to indicate no contest at all.

JOHANSSON vs PATTERSON

Next we look at a heavyweight world title match that pitted Ingemar Johansson against Floyd Patterson. The Ascendant on this chart is over the 28 degrees, but the chart is a fine one to demonstrate another interpretation of the aspects in a contest chart. Here they describe the psychological implications and their influence upon behavior which lead to a loss.

The question posed was, "Will Johansson defeat Patterson in the world title match?" The chart was set for June 16, 1960, 34N04 118W15, at 10:41 A.M. Pacific Daylight Time.

Cusps: MC 24 ♉ 22, 11th 27 ♊ 52, 12th 29 ♋ 29, ASC 28 ♌ 11, 2nd 22 ♍ 43, and 3rd 21 ♎ 43.

Planetary positions:

Zodiac	Declination		Zodiac	Declination
☉ 25♊33	22N20		♄ 16♑35Rx	22S00
☽ 02♈07	02S12		♅ 18♌09	16N03
☿ 20♋12	22N57		♆ 06♏37Rx	12S02
♀ 23♊56	23N28		♀ 03♍51	21N33
♂ 27♈20	09N21		MC 24♉22	18N52
♃ 29♐10Rx	23S07		ASC 28♌11	12N07

Johansson's side of the chart (east) shows the rulers of his tenth house cusp (Taurus) and first house cusp (Leo) to be Venus and the Sun - both located in his house of honor. Because Pluto is ruler of Patterson's tenth house of honor (the fourth in this chart) and is positioned in Johansson's first house, it would seem that Johansson had a certain control over Patterson. But it takes more than that to indicate a win.

With Aquarius on the seventh cusp (Patterson's prowess), we look to the co-rulers: Uranus appears on Johansson's side, and Saturn occupies a position on Patterson's side.

Checking out the two malefics (Saturn and Mars), we find them both on Patterson's side. The benefics are split: Jupiter on Patterson's side and Venus on Johansson's. Furthermore, the planetary distribution by side is close - six to four in slight favor of Johansson.

At this point let us look for a different factor in the sides - the state of mind of the contestants. Johansson's is mapped by the third house where we find Neptune in the sign of Scorpio. Neptune is inconjunct with the Moon, general ruler of the subconscious mind. This combination represents a wavering of decision and an oversensitive trend.

Venus, ruler of Libra, in Johansson's house of honor (the tenth) is opposing Jupiter in the fifth house of hazards. This aspect reinforces the sensitivity and also hints of a loss of control which could become a detriment in executing his skill.

Pluto, in his first house, is inconjunct that Jupiter in the fifth house signifying a tendency to become agitated or to become overcautious to the point that it prevents clear thinking (a must in the fight game). Adding to this state of mind is the potential mapped by the Sun opposing Jupiter, overconfidence.

The ninth house governs Patterson's state of mind. Here we see a different picture. Even though Mars will oppose Neptune, Mars is trine Jupiter and sextile the Sun. These patterns map a certain confidence and courage that is often found in winners. Because Mars is past the square aspect with Mercury in his fifth house of hazards (the eleventh house in this chart), his obstacles appear to be behind him.

Rocky Marciano, the undefeated ex-champion at the time, watched the fight from ringside. He said, "The fight isn't a minute old and I'm saying to the guys around me that Johansson is going to get killed. I was saying this because I was looking at Patterson's face. He was having a helluva time for himself. He loved every move and fake and punch of the fight. He was alert and he kept changing his moves continually. Johansson didn't know where the punches were coming from."

Outcome: Patterson knocked Johansson out in the fifth round.

Aside from winning the honor in such bouts, the purse is also important. Johansson's money house (the second - his purse) is ruled by Mercury because Virgo appears on the house cusp. Mercury is opposition Saturn - the opponent. Saturn rules the seventh cusp - Patterson's first house. Patterson's money (the eighth in this chart) has Neptune as co-ruler of Pisces on the cusp. His gain of the purse is shown by Neptune sextile Pluto (his honor and ruler of the fourth house).

LOUIS VS. WALCOTT

None of the chart interpretations explained in this chapter have been given in detail. Highlights have been explored to better comprehend the approach in delineating contest charts.

However, examples of the most important factors in judging such charts have been demonstrated so that the reader should be able to make out the significance of his own charts.

Now the next chart of the Joe Louis vs. Joe Walcott is a favorite for use in demonstrating this technique, because the outcome is so clearly evident. At the time the fight took place there had been much talk about whether Joe Louis would continue to retain his heavyweight title. That was the main topic of conversation wherever fight fans gathered, because popular opinion favored Walcott to win and take the title away from Louis.

Will Joe Louis win?" The chart was set for December 5, 1947, 34N04 118W15, at 6:15 A.M. Pacific Standard Time.

Cusps: MC 18 ♍ 05, 11th 18 ♎ 46, 12th 14 ♏ 03, ASC 05 ♐ 39, 2nd 07 ♑ 07, and 3rd 12 ♒ 35.

Planetary positions:

Zodiac	Declination		Zodiac	Declination
☉ 12 ♐ 36	22S18		♄ 22 ♌ 40StaRx	14N57
☽ 19 ♍ 48	08N21		♅ 22 ♊ 36Rx	23N29
☿ 26 ♏ 49	18S18		♆ 12 ♎ 33	03S35
♀ 06 ♑ 07	24S34		♀ 14 ♌ 52	23N17
♂ 01 ♍ 25	13N17		MC 18 ♍ 05	04N43
♃ 09 ♐ 18	21S19		ASC 05 ♐ 39	21S15

After all that talk and excitement and the numbers quoted by odds makers, it was hard to believe what the chart indicated. Louis will win. It was even more difficult to trust that answer as the bout got underway. The fight went 15 rounds, and Louis was knocked down twice. Although Walcott received the most points, two of the three judges picked Louis as the winner. The public was against the decision, but the chart proved to be correct. The 1-2-3 of contest charts had given the right answer.

Dividing the chart: Louis is represented by the east side, and Walcott by the west. Louis has more planets on his side, as well as the two benefics - Jupiter and Venus. The rulers of his first and tenth houses are also on his side of the chart.

Walcott's side shows fewer planets, as well as both malefics - Mars and Saturn. The ruler of his first house (the seventh in this chart), Mercury, is located on Louis' side, and the co-rulers of Pisces, which appears on Walcott's tenth house (the fourth here) are in Louis' houses of honor (Neptune) and personal prowess (Jupiter) - showing that Louis has complete control of the situation in spite of the odds against him.

Walcott has only one important ruler, Uranus, on his side. On the other hand, aside from the patterns mentioned above, Louis' luck factor should be noticed.

Louis' side shows only two more planets than Walcott's. But look at their house positions and aspects. Five of the six planets are in angular houses, mapping strength. And they are involved in trines and sextiles - aspects denoting a luck factor.

3. SPORTS GAMES

Highlighting the winter sports fans' holiday season are the various football games played on New Year's Day. The Rose Bowl Game at Pasadena, California, is probably the best known.However, there are four others that receive wide attention on this holiday. They are the Fiesta Bowl at Tempe, Arizona; the Cotton Bowl at Dallas, Texas; the Orange Bowl at Miami, Florida; and the Sugar Bowl at New Orleans, Louisiana. These bowl games provide excellent opportunities to test the contest chart technique. Before timing one of these game charts, it is essential that the person asking the question have an intense desire to know the answer about some one thing. More than one question asked at the same time brings a multiple birth of mental events, resulting in imperfect births. If there is not a deep desire to know one answer, the mental event does not have sufficient vitality to live, and therefore the unexpected results are not apt to be realized.

Clear, directed thinking helps to define a single, strong question. The erroneous approach here would be to ask several other questions at the same time, such as: Will the game be a shutout? Will the star pitcher produce a no-hitter? Will Mr. X break the records for batting in homers? Will Mr. Z get the longest run of the season?

After analyzing many contests, it was found that in games in which there is little interest the result obtained in picking a winner was just about what would be attained through chance. But where there is much interest, the question should be asked relative to the team which one desires to win, or about which at least there is the most interest. Do not ask: Will such and such a team beat X team? Instead, ask: Will my favorite team be the winner?

Although a true sports fan watches all the preliminary games throughout the football season, usually he comes to associate himself with one team. By the time the Rose Bowl game comes around, and especially if his team is one of the participants, he is well qualified to ask if his team will win. The strong desire-energy behind his question will give a clear chart that ought to be easy to read. Why? Because the mental factors about ONE thing are pushed strongly to the forefront of his mind. Will my team win? A simple, clear, definite question.

ROSE BOWL PLAYOFF

The querent of this first chart had been following the scores and plays of the Oregon State football team. spHe was delighted when the team earned the honor of being one of the contestants in 1958 against Ohio State at the Rose Bowl.

He asked, "Will Oregon State win the Rose Bowl Game?" The chart was cast for January 1, 1958, 34N04 118W15, at 3:02 P.M. Pacific Standard Time before the game ended.

Cusps: MC 26 ≈ 03, 11th 28 ✕ 00, 12th 07 ♉ 06, ASC 16 ♊ 00, 2nd 08 ♋ 46, and 3rd 00 ♌ 52.

Planetary positions:

Zodiac	Declination	Zodiac	Declination
☉ 11 ♑ 03	22S59	♄ 19 ♐ 33	21S42
☽ 22 ♉ 57	17N12	♅ 10 ♌ 47Rx	18N10
☿ 26 ♐ 11Rx	20S13	♆ 04 ♏ 27	11S22
♀ 15 ≈ 33	15S12	♀ 02 ♍ 08	21N34
♂ 06 ♐ 52	21S24	MC 26 ≈ 03	12S51
♃ 28 ♎ 43	09S50	ASC 16 ♊ 00	22N42

In a question of this type the querent steps aside and has no position in the chart. The wheel is divided into two contending parts: The six houses on the east side of the wheel represent the team asked about, or the favorite; and the six houses on the west side picture the opposing team. Here, the east side represents Oregon State, and the west side stands for Ohio state.

First, let us consider the location of the planets. Because the majority of them occupy the west half of the horoscope, all things being equal, we say that in a general way the opposing Ohio team has more power -- more planets appear on their side.

The nature of the planets also enters into the general judging. Planets are classed three ways: (1) Harmonious: Jupiter and Venus. (2) Inharmonious: Saturn and Mars. (3) Neutral: Sun, Moon, Mercury, Uranus, Neptune and Pluto.

When harmonious, or benefic planets, appear on one side of the chart, they favor the team which that side represents. And if the inharmonious, or malefic, planets appear on one side, they indicate obstacles to overcome for the team represented by that side. In this particular chart, both malefics and benefics are located on the west side, or Ohio, side of the wheel. That fact, if not synthesized with all of the other factors in the horoscope, would lead us to believe that Ohio would experience both good and bad luck during the game.

In addition to this general appraisal, we have to see how much control each team has over itself and its own honor. The team itself is ruled by the first house, which also pictures its ability and technique. The team's honor is represented by the tenth house. In this chart, the first and tenth houses tell how much control Oregon has over itself and its honor. On the other hand, the seventh and fourth houses signify how much control Ohio will have over itself and its honor.

Gemini rising on the first house cusp (the Oregon team) is ruled by Mercury which is found in the seventh house (the Ohio team), indicating that Ohio "controls" Oregon. Aquarius on the tenth cusp (Oregon's honor) is co-ruled by Uranus and Saturn. Uranus is posited on Oregon's side and Saturn occupies Ohio's side. With Saturn in the seventh house (Ohio's ability), Ohio "controls" Oregon's honor.

Aside from being ruled by Saturn and Mercury in the seventh house, the Ohio team is also ruled by Jupiter because Sagittarius occupies the house cusp. Jupiter is on Ohio's (west) side of the chart, reinforcing the fact that the Ohio team "controls" itself.

Ohio's honor (fourth house), in addition to Pluto in that house, is ruled by the Sun (which rules Leo on the fourth house cusp) and is found on the west (Ohio) side, emphasizing again that Ohio has "control" over its own honor.

Outcome: Ohio State came out ahead with a score of 10 to 7. Even though it was a close game, perhaps two astrological factors mapped the small difference in the score. The malefics -- Saturn and Mars -- being located on Ohio's side. From a glance at this chart, it is easy to see that the favored team of Oregon State would lose the bowl game. All of the important luck and power factors occupy Ohio State's side of the horoscope.

WORLD SERIES GAMES

Many other team sporting events are held every month of the year. Competitive teams -- both amateur and professional -- in basketball, hockey, bowling, tennis, polo, soccer, etc. vie for the highest honors.

Football is most popular in the United States, soccer captures the fans' attention abroad, and if the gate receipts determine popularity, then baseball is one of the top sports in this country as well. The most honored and talked-of sport event of the year aside from the bowl games is the World Series which has been played annually since 1905. That great event is usually held in October each year.

In 1957, the World Series Games pitted the New York Yankees against the Milwaukee Braves. After six games, the series was all tied up -- three games each. On the day the last game was played, a group of us were working on some astrological research material. We got to talking about the series as it came over the air. (You'd think we were all Geminis, because we did our work and listened to the game at the same time.) There was so much talk that I had an ESP -- a strong one -- that the Braves would win.

Due to the fact that the Milwaukee Braves had never won the pennant, in the good old American style, we were all rooting for the underdog to win. The question was: "Will the Milwaukee Braves win the 1957 World Series?" The chart was set for 9:59 a.m. Pacific Standard Time, on October 10, 1957, at 34N04 118W15.

Cusps: MC 19 ♍ 44, 11th 20 ♎ 20, 12th 15 ♏ 22, ASC 06 ♐ 48, 2nd 08 ♑ 36, and 3rd 14 ♒ 14.

Planetary positions:

Zodiac	Declination	Zodiac	Declination
☉ 17♎10	06S33	♄ 10 ♐25	20S33
☽ 07 ♉45	12N46	♅ 11 ♌02	18N04
☿ 07♎27	01S40	♆ 01♏46	10S29
♀ 00 ♐48	22S32	♀ 01 ♍36	21N18
♂ 10♎47	03S40	MC 19♍44	04N04
♃ 13♎15	09S14	ASC 06 ♐48	21S27

As soon as we looked at the chart we knew the answer. Sometimes it takes more time to set up the chart than to read it. The first house (the seventh here) of ability and the tenth house (the fourth here) of honor for the New York Yankees are vacant -- no planets there mapped a lack of energy. No energy, no action.

Let's take it step by step, just the way you will read your own charts when asking about a baseball team winning a game. I hope you will, it is a great experience and a neat way to learn more astrology. And it beats puzzles by a mile for genuine fun.

Drawing the mental line vertically through this wheel from top to bottom, we immediately see that seven of the ten planets appear on the Brave's side. Both malefic planets, Mars and Saturn, are there, but they are in close sextile aspect from the first house (Brave's prowess) to the tenth house (their honor). The sextile aspect usually represents an opportunity for luck, but the discordant nature of the malefic planets detracts to some extent from the full harmonious power.

The ruler of the Ascendant is Jupiter. It appears in the Brave's own tenth house of honor. Therefore, with the other benefic (Venus) in conjunction aspect with the Ascendant, the Braves would seem to be in complete control of the situation.

The Yankees, on the other hand, show only three planets on their side, and none of them occupy angular houses -- especially the seventh (their ability) and the fourth (their honor). This indicates little power -- perhaps not enough to win.

Mercury, ruler of their house of ability, is in the Brave's tenth house, and Jupiter, ruler of the Yankee's honor house is also in the Brave's tenth house. This placement of planets shows that the Braves have the Yankees in their power.

As the game got into action, this did not appear to be so. The pictured Saturn-Mars energy-release maps the obstacles which popped up in the first part of the game. However after that, there was smooth sailing for the Braves, who came through to win in the end. And what a win! The underdog, the Milwaukee Braves, had accomplished what no one thought they could do. Onlookers cheered them as they carried the pennant at the 1957 World Series.

As a means of enlightening comparison, look back at the Rose Bowl chart where the favored team lost. A comparison of the two charts will make it easier to judge contest charts to find who will win a game.

1958 BRAVES vs YANKEES

Another graphic chart concerning the next year's World Series was set at 7:42 p.m. Pacific Standard Time, for September 30, 1958, 34N04 118W15. Question: "Will the Braves win the 1958 World Series?"

Cusps: MC 04 ≈ 10, 11th 02 ⌧ 03, 12th 08 ♈ 48, ASC 21 ♉ 47, 2nd 18 ♊ 36, and 3rd 11 ♋ 05.

Planetary positions:

Zodiac	Declination	Zodiac	Declination
☉ 07 ♎ 28	02S46	♄ 20 ♐ 15	21S57
☽ 12 ♉ 37	12N34	♅ 15 ♌ 11	16N53
☿ 04 ♎ 01	01N30	♆ 03 ♏ 33	11S05
♀ 26 ♍ 50	02N39	♀ 03 ♍ 14	21N00
♂ 01 ♊ 56	18N52	MC 04 ≈ 10	19S13
♃ 04 ♏ 38	12S07	ASC 21 ♉ 47	18N11

To capture the World Series pennant, a baseball team is required to win four out of seven games. Sometimes not all seven games have to be played. One team could take four games straight, one right after the other, to become champ. In this particular contest all seven games had to be played.

Going into the contest, each team had won three games and needed one more to come out on top. After inspecting this chart, you shouldn't have to study it very long to come up with the correct conclusion that the favored team (the east side) lost the championship and the Yankees walked away with the pennant.

Almost all of the planets appear on the Yankee's side of the chart which also holds the planetary rulers of the tenth house and the first house of the Braves. Uranus and Saturn rule the Brave's house of honor (tenth), because Aquarius occupies the Midheaven. Venus rules their ability, because Taurus is rising on the cusp of the first house.

The Brave's side (east) shows very little power in the honor house (no planets there), and with Mars in the first house, they acted out its indications. When the game started, they rushed out onto the field ready to give the game their all. But that rush really acted as a show, because it fizzled out as they met one obstacle after another. Finally, they ran out of steam and seemed to merely put in their time until the game came to an end.

Even though Mars is a member of a grand trine with Mercury conjunction the Sun in the fifth house of hazards and the Midheaven, they could not keep up the pace. This grand trine falls in air signs, so it is little wonder that they made so many false moves and frittered away what energy they had stored away for the game.

A deceptive knot of conceit may have presented a mental bar for they had won the Series the year before. Perhaps the grand trine, mapping overconfidence and a lack of enduring enthusiasm and energy when something went wrong acted as a detriment to the expression of their ability. The psychological impact added to their lack of power (only two planets on their side) tells the story.

The same rules may be used with success in judging charts cast for other team efforts like sculling or boat racing teams, such as Cowe's Regatta, or even game shows like Family Feud, and television competitions like Star Search.

4. POLITICAL ELECTIONS

Cosmodynes are the result of applying a simple mathematical yardstick to all chart elements in order to obtain complete chart synthesis, which is difficult at best when using the physical brain alone to blend these myriad influences.

Not only is the power and nature of each planet, sign, house and aspect brought into the equation, the relation of the strength of the house as well as planetary locations within the house as measured by strength, harmony, and discord is embraced in the final tabulation. The foundation for this process is explained in How to Read Cosmodynes.[1]

We chose not to include the cosmodynes with all of these contest charts to keep the rules as simple and clear as possible. However, when we do include cosmodynes in the study of a contest chart, we arrive at a much closer estimate of each factor in the horoscope as it relates to the winner or winning team.

The outstanding effective use of cosmodynes (astrodynes, harmodynes and discordynes -- measurements of power, harmony and discord) was graphically demonstrated back in 1948 when Truman opposed Dewey for the Presidency of the United States. Everyone was sure that Dewey would win the election. Yet, one astrologer who applied the cosmodyne technique was sure that Truman would be victorious.

Even as the votes were being counted, it appeared that Dewey would win the election. One New York newspaper was so sure of it that they published a huge headline proclaiming that Dewey had won in their morning newspaper. That headline was a little premature.

When the country awakened to a new day after the election, their radios were broadcasting a victory for Harry S. Truman. The final count: Truman -- 24,105,812 popular votes and 303 electoral votes. Thomas E. Dewey -- 21,970,065 popular votes and 189 electoral votes.

Astrologer Elbert Benjamine, who employed astrodynes to make a determination, was one of the few who said that Truman would win. The reason the cosmodyne approach works so well is because the tenth house in a contest chart is the most powerful to attract a win. The precision offered by calculating the cosmodynes is a splendid and accurate measurement for use in the contest technique.

Before setting up the contest chart and calculating the cosmodynes, another important factor should be considered. That is the proper timing of the question. More readable contest charts are encouraged by providing the proper physical and astral environment to aid the subconscious mind in assembling and arranging the pertinent factors necessary to provide a descriptive astral pattern of the situation.

To provide such an all-inclusive environment, the question should be timed for when there is a strong desire to know who will win only after both candidates have been named.

CALIFORNIA GOVERNOR'S RACE

After the candidates were named, the question was asked: "Will Nixon defeat Brown for the governorship?" The chart was erected for June 7, 1962, 34N04 118W15, at 7:19 p.m. Pacific Daylight Time.

Cusps: MC 21 ♍ 19, 11th 22 ♎ 12, 12th 17 ♏ 02, ASC 08 ♐ 35, 2nd 10 ♑ 28, and 3rd 16 ♒ 19.

Planetary positions:

Zodiac	Declination		Zodiac	Declination
☉ 16 ♊ 50	22N47		♄ 11 ♒ 10Rx	18S00
☽ 23 ♌ 03	14N55		♅ 26 ♌ 55	13N14
☿ 15 ♊ 42Rx	19N41		♆ 11 ♏ 13Rx	13S28
♀ 19 ♋ 09	23N52		♀ 07 ♍ 37	20N53
♂ 07 ♉ 31	13N16		MC 21 ♍ 49	03N15
♃ 11 ♓ 45	08S07		ASC 08 ♐ 35	21S44

As Nixon was asked about, he is represented by the east side of the chart. His honor (the tenth house) is signified by Mercury because Mercury rules Virgo on the tenth house cusp. Mercury is located in Brown's first house (the seventh here). This indicates that Brown has a certain control over Nixon's honor.

Now look at Brown's tenth house (the fourth house in this chart). The co-rulers of Pisces on the house cusp are Neptune and Jupiter, both of which appear on Nixon's side of the chart. Some loss of Brown's control over his own honor is mapped by this placement.

Both of the benefics planets -- Jupiter and Venus -- and the malefic planets -- Saturn and Mars -- are split by side locations. Saturn and Jupiter occupy Nixon's side, while Mars and Venus are placed on Brown's side.

As far as judging this chart for a winner, the above is just so-so. Nothing definitive. Two outstanding indications, though, determine who won that contest. One is that Brown's side holds both the Sun and Mercury in his house of ability; and two, that Brown has more strength in general on his side -- seven of the ten planets appear there.

Every aspect in a contest chart maps situations and conditions related to the contest. However, here the opposition between Mars and Neptune was descriptive of some of Nixon's motives for running for this public office. These motives were plainly evident to the voters and had much to do with his defeat.

The year before this question was asked (1961), the Democrats had ousted the Republicans from the White house. At the time, Nixon had just completed a term as Vice President under Eisenhower. So he was left without a job and out of the public eye.

That Mars-Neptune opposition aspect describes his motive behind his action. He no doubt agreed with the former Vice President the first two terms of Franklin Delano Roosevelt's Presidency, John Nance Garner, who said that being Vice President was as "effective as a pitcher of warm spit."

Nixon wanted the top spot. He ran for the governorship of one of the largest states in the Union as a stepping stone to the Presidency.

Although he was defeated by Brown, six years later he was elected President of the United States and then reelected in 1972.

STEVENSON vs EISENHOWER

1956 was the year of a heated political campaign. Adlai E. Stevenson was the favorite of the intellectuals and eggheads, while Eisenhower was the multiple-honored and decorated army general whose movements had been explicitly chronicled worldwide.

That atmosphere prompted the question, "Will Adlai E. Stevenson win the presidential election?" The chart was cast for October 30, 1956, 34N04 118W15, at 11:29 p.m. Pacific Standard Time.

Cusps: MC 5 ♉ 53, 11th 10 ♊ 28, 12th 13 ♋ 25, ASC 12 ♌ 59, 2nd 06 ♍ 02, and 3rd 03 ♎ 33.

Planetary positions:

Zodiac	Declination	Zodiac	Declination
☉ 07 ♏ 51	14S08	♄ 02 ♐ 11	18S55
☽ 07 ♎ 45	06S50	♅ 06 ♌ 55	19N07
☿ 29 ♎ 57	10S16	♆ 00 ♏ 29	10S03
♀ 29 ♍ 24	01N36	♀ 00 ♍ 12	21N31
♂ 15 ♓ 54	07S40	MC 05 ♉ 53	13N29
♃ 22 ♍ 44	03N28	ASC 12 ♌ 59	16N55

Here Stevenson is represented by the east side of the chart, and his opponent (Dwight D. Eisenhower) is mapped by the west side. This particular chart is not as clearcut as the others, but the weight of power and luck are definitely pictured.

Stevenson has more planets on his side, as well as the two benefics -- Jupiter and Venus. But the Sun, ruling his first house (ability) is located in Ike's tenth (the fourth here), indicating that Ike had a certain amount of control over Stevenson's luck. Venus, ruler of Stevenson's tenth house (honor) is on his own side of the wheel, but he does not have any planets (strength) in the tenth house of honor.

Even though Eisenhower had only three planets on his side -- two of them malefics, his tenth is powerful, containing not only a co-ruler of his own Ascendant (Saturn, as Aquarius is on the seventh cusp) but the ruler of Stevenson's Ascendant (Sun, as Leo is rising). Also on his own side is the ruler of the tenth cusp -- Mars. That

Stevenson lost the presidential election is signified by his extremely weak tenth house -- a factor of much importance in judging contest charts.

A tally of the final vote gave Adlai E. Stevenson 26,031,322 popular votes and 73 electoral votes, and Dwight D. Eisenhower was given 35,585,316 popular votes and 457 electoral votes.

JOHNSON vs GOLDWATER

Another presidential contest chart shows a fairly even distribution of factors on each side, but when that important tenth house is active on one side and not on the other, that energetic side wins more often than not.

This chart was probably not the result of asking for the outcome at the appropriate time for there is no obvious indication of the winner. "Will Lyndon B. Johnson defeat Barry Goldwater for the U.S. Presidency?" The chart was cast for November 2, 1964, 34N04 118W15, at 10:10 a.m. Pacific Standard Time.

Cusps: MC 17 ♎ 40, 11th 14 ♏ 57, 12th 07 ♐ 43, ASC 29 ♐ 18, 2nd 04 ♒ 57, and 3rd 13 ♓ 32.

Planetary positions:

Zodiac	Declination	Zodiac	Declination
☉ 10 ♏ 21	14S56	♄ 28 ♒ 21	13S37
☽ 22 ♎ 29	04S33	♅ 13 ♍ 49	07N03
☿ 21 ♏ 22	19S09	♆ 17 ♏ 18	15S22
♀ 02 ♎ 52	00N18	♀ 15 ♍ 46	18N21
♂ 28 ♌ 12	13N39	MC 17 ♎ 40	06S56
♃ 22 ♉ 28Rx	17N11	ASC 29 ♐ 18	23S27

An even distribution is what the first glance at the horoscope reveals -- five planets on each side. Johnson has two planets located in his house of honor (tenth), while Goldwater has none in his (fourth house). Neither contestant has planets placed in his house of ability (first and seventh houses). The rulers of these houses -- Jupiter and Mercury -- are situated on opposite sides of the wheel. The malefics are split by side location; and the benefics are located in Goldwater's side.

-31-

All the pertinent factors for judging the outcome seem to balance each other out except two. The benefics appear on Goldwater's side. But, alone, they do not make up for the strength seen on Johnson's side -- that is the power of the honor house (tenth). Johnson's honor is much stronger than Goldwater's. That strength would far exceed anything else if the cosmodynes had been applied.

Outcome: Lyndon B. Johnson won the 1964 U.S. Presidential election with 43,126,506 popular votes and 486 electoral votes. Goldwater was defeated. He had less than half of the popular vote, 27,176,799 and only 52 electoral votes.

CONGRESSIONAL CONTEST

Shirley Temple was an outstanding movie star in the 1930's. But as she grew into her teens, the roles she played were less endearing to the public. Later, after her marriage to business executive Charles A. Black, she entered public service with the same enthusiasm as she had shown as a child.

She decided to run for a U.S. Congressional seat. Naturally the media spread the word far and wide, and she became the talk of the nation once more. This inspired one of her fans to ask, "Will Shirley Temple Black win a congressional seat?" The chart was cast for November 19, 1967, 34N04 118W42, at 5:51 p.m. Pacific Standard Time.

Cusps: MC 24 ≈ 08, 11th 25 ✕ 42, 12th 04 ♉ 52, ASC 14 ♊ 17, 2nd 07 ♋ 13, and 3rd 29 ♋ 12.

Planetary positions:

Zodiac	Declination	Zodiac	Declination
☉ 27 ♏ 03	19S30	♄ 05 ♈ 59Rx	00S01
☽ 28 ♊ 48	28N01	♅ 28 ♍ 17	01N22
☿ 07 ♏ 55	12S00	♆ 24 ♏ 12	17S12
♀ 10 ♎ 49	02S46	♀ 22 ♍ 30	16N38
♂ 20 ♑ 58	21S17	MC 24 ≈ 08	22N31
♃ 04 ♍ 13	10N48	ASC 14 ♊ 17	13S29

Many constituents knew her as the little darling dancer on the Good Ship Lollypop. They were uninformed as to her civic, community and political activities both in Washington and California. That and the fact that she ran against nine other candidates, all men, for a seat in the House of Representatives from California's Eleventh District (San Francisco area) had much to do with her defeat.

This chart shows all but two planets on the side of the opposition. Also, the strength, when comparing the houses of honor (tenth and fourth), supports the opposition. Jupiter and Pluto appear in the fourth house (the opposition's honor). The Sun, ruling the fourth house cusp, is located on the opponent's side of the wheel.

One of the factors associated with her defeat was her reputation as explained above. In addition, her friends (eleventh house) were not as supportive as they could have been. Saturn, in the eleventh house of friends, opposes Venus in the sixth house of hazards. Note that Saturn rules the Midheaven sign of Aquarius -- her reputation and honor. Political observers disagreed as to how much influence her childhood reputation had on the election -- Neptune parallel the Midheaven.

Outcome: Shirley Temple Black was defeated by Republican Paul N. McClosky, although she won more votes than two other Republicans and six Democrats.

In Chapter 7, there are more charts of political contests which can be compared to those in this chapter for study purposes.

5. ONE AGAINST THE FIELD

In many contests there are more than two participants who are not a team. Two or more contestants are involved in athletic competitions like the Olympics or figure skating pairs championships; auto races like Le Mans or the Indiana 500; talent contests such as televisions's Star Search; and horse races, such as the Kentucky Derby or Epsom Downs.

Divided opinions have been offered as to how an astrologer should interpret the charts set on questions for these events. Some say that the use of the contest rules will give a clear answer. Others claim that an ordinary horary chart, with the Moon assigned as co-ruler of the Ascendant, can be employed effectively if the contestant asks the question himself.

Environment, proper wording, and timing are important in making a decision as to which interpretive approach to use to judge the chart. In order to demonstrate the two approaches, let us consider the plight of the ...

CONTEST WIDOW

Boxes were spilling off of cupboard shelves, and the drawers would not close they were so full of stuff she would not use. Hands on hips, Mrs. Bell stood in the middle of her kitchen about to blow her top. Harry was at it again! If he bought one more box and tore off the top, she would scream. Although he had been contesting for years, he had never won a thing. Today he had started a contest puzzle instead of doing the things around the place that needed to be done. Mrs. Bell was sure that he was wasting his time.

In the middle of her frustration, she asked, "Will he win this one?" You see, Harry had told her earlier that he had a strong hunch this was the one he would win. Her question timed the chart: December 5, 1957, 34N34 118W15, at 6:13 p.m. Pacific Standard Time.

Cusps: MC 29 ♓ 09, 11th 04 ♐ 34, 12th 11 ♊ 24, ASC 14 ♋ 23, 2nd 05 ♌ 34, and 3rd 29 ♌ 45.

Planetary positions:

Zodiac	Declination	Zodiac	Declination
☉ 24 ♐ 52	23N18	♄ 17 ♐ 37	21S32
☽ 18 ♎ 05	08S48	♅ 11 ♌ 17Rx	18N01
☿ 11 ♑ 31	23S37	♆ 04 ♏ 05	11S15
♀ 07 ♒ 17	20S06	♀ 02 ♍ 17Rx	21N25
♂ 25 ♏ 12	18S51	MC 29 ♓ 09	00S21
♃ 26 ♎ 19	09S03	ASC 14 ♋ 23	22N41

Following the contest chart rules, Harry is represented by the east side of the chart, and all of the other contestants in the field are indicated by the west side. Just a glance at the "widow" chart tells us we need not tarry long over the 1-2-3 to get an answer.

The opposition has most of the planets, including both benefics and malefics as well as all of the rulers of Harry's honor (tenth house) and ability (first house). Harry didn't have a chance. He lost the contest. When he received the news he didn't seem to mind his loss, because he was busy trying to flatten an unusually-shaped bottle top so that he could put it into an envelope with an entry blank.

Next, we look at this same chart from the horary angle: "Will my husband win the contest?" is the proper wording for the horary chart.

First, we establish the important houses and their rulers.

Her husband is mapped by the seventh house, which becomes his first house. His ruler is Saturn, because Capricorn occupies the house cusp and no planets are situated in the house. His honor is mapped by the fourth house in this chart, which becomes his tenth house when counting around from the seventh house. Saturn falls in his twelfth house (the sixth here).

As Harry is not the one asking the question, he is not mapped by the first house or the Moon. In the contest horary rules, the querent steps aside. If Mrs. Bell had asked the question about herself winning, then the first house and the Moon would rule her. But in this type of question, she has no place in the wheel except to establish her relationship with the person asked about.

Reading this wheel from the horary standpoint, we have to judge if there are applying aspects tying Harry and his honor together in the future. His honor (represented here by the fourth house) is strong as it holds three planets -- the Moon, Jupiter and Neptune. These planets rule the house, but we must also include Mercury (for Virgo on the house cusp) and Venus (for the intercepted sign of Libra) as co-rulers.

Saturn (Harry) is separating from sextiles to the Moon and Jupiter. These connections signify past situations and activity because the aspects have already formed.

In order to signal a win, the rulers of his ability (seventh house) and his honor (fourth house) should be applying by aspect, bringing the querent (Harry) and the quesited (a win) together. Apart from an applying aspect of this type, there should be enough strength and harmony to fortify the support shown by the applying aspect(s). With no such support or indication shown in this horary chart, it matches his loss of the contest.

As we have seen, in this particular case both the contest chart and the horary technique resulted in the same answer. Could this be true of judging all charts calculated where one is contending against a field of many entrants?

SWEEPSTAKES AND LOTTERIES

These techniques applied above can be tested on situations where ability more than luck is required to win a contest. Examples are seen in answering a given question in twenty-five words or less, or the trivial pursuit type of contest where a keen memory is an asset. The rules can be applied also to situations where chance and luck alone determine the winner, such as in raffles, drawings, lotteries, or sweepstakes.

Never having entered a sweepstakes game, we were forced to research just how they are handled. We learned that tickets are sold up to a cutoff date. Then in a contest, such as the Irish Sweepstakes, the tickets are drawn one by one for each horse appearing in the race. The holders of the tickets drawn are notified as to which horse their ticket represents.

If the horse happens to be a favorite, the ticket immediately becomes valuable. Some of these tickets have been sold for a quarter of a million dollars BEFORE the race is even run! It would be at the time that the tickets were allotted that a valid horary question could be asked about the result. A passing thought pops up; it would be sad to refuse $250,000 for your ticket before the race, when the day after it might be a worthless piece of paper.

Once the race has been run, the payoffs go to those tickets representing the WIN, PLACE, AND SHOW horses. All others end up in the trash can.

Lotteries also involve enormous numbers of people. Since New Hampshire started the first modern lottery in 1964, the idea has met with great resistance. But one by one the States began to sanction a lottery. Now twenty years later, there are 17 States plus Puerto Rico and the District of Columbia which have gotten into the action. Now there is talk about going one step further -- an official United States lottery held nationwide.

In these state lotteries, numbers rather than horses are used to select the winners. In either case, there are millions of people looking to win. On January, 1983 the estimated resident United States population was 232.6 million people. These facts point to high odds of winning, which some claim to be 3,000,000 to 1.

With 50 million Americans interested in astrology, these lottery contests should provide plenty of fascinating research. There are no lottery charts in this chapter. However, the same delineation approaches as applied to sweepstakes charts can be applied in analyzing lottery charts.

IRISH SWEEPSTAKES

In 1961 two charts were erected by my students for questions about the same event -- one by the contestant himself, and one by a friend of the contestant.

The Irish Hospital's Sweepstakes was to be run at Newmarket, England. The friend asked: "Will my friend win the sweepstakes?" The chart was cast for June 16, 1961, 34N04 118W15, at 2:16 p.m. Pacific Daylight Time.

Cusps: MC 19 ♋ 04, 11th 21 ♌ 35, 12th 21 ♍ 29, ASC 17 ♎ 22, 2nd 15 ♏ 26, and 3rd 16 ♐ 21.

Planetary positions:

Zodiac	Declination		Zodiac	Declination
☉ 25 ♊ 27	23N22		♄ 28 ♑ 44Rx	20S31
☽ 06 ♌ 26	16N41		♅ 22 ♌ 40	14N38
☿ 10 ♋ 16Rx	21N20		♆ 08 ♏ 51Rx	12S43
♀ 09 ♉ 48	12N03		♇ 05 ♍ 46	21N14
♂ 22 ♌ 57	14N49		MC 19 ♋ 04	22N05
♃ 06 ♒ 23Rx	19S10		ASC 17 ♎ 22	06S49

Important houses to consider here are those ruling the querent when we take the horary approach. The wording of the question determines which houses in the horary chart are emphasized. "Will" implies the future. Therefore any action indicated in the chart would be mapped by an applying aspect which ties the planets of the important houses to one another.

"My friend" tells us that the person asking the question is not involved in the outcome, as he is not asking the question about himself. He steps aside. The friend is mapped by the eleventh house, and that house is considered the first house of the friend. If we count forward from that house to his fifth house of speculation (the sweepstakes), we arrive at the third house in this wheel.

"Win the sweepstakes" are words that point to the friend's tenth house, which is the eighth house in this chart, after counting forward from the friend's first house (the eleventh here). With Taurus on the cusp of the eighth house, Venus rules the friend's honor (the eighth). Going back to the third house here (his speculation house) we note that Jupiter rules Sagittarius on the house cusp.

Taking these three important areas into consideration, an indication of future activity would be mapped by an applying aspect between Jupiter, Venus, or his planetary rulers, which are Uranus, Mars and Pluto (located in his first house -- the eleventh in this chart). Because Leo occupies the house cusp, the Sun is also one of his rulers.

The only aspects involving all of these planets are separating: Venus trine Pluto, and Jupiter inconjunct Pluto. They match the fact that he did not win as the aspects indicate something in the past and not in his future.

Now if we apply the contest rules, he would be mapped by the first house and the east side of the chart. This house is ruled by Neptune (in the house) and Venus (ruling Libra on the cusp) as well as the Ascendant. His honor (tenth house) is ruled by the Moon because it is stationed in the house and also rules Cancer on the house cusp. The Midheaven aspects will also play a part in the delineation of the tenth house. Venus is placed on the opponents' side, signifying that the contestant's ability (first house) is affected by the opposition.

Both sides show an even number of planets located in the houses, but the opposition not only has a stronger tenth house (the fourth here), there is a lot of luck mapped on that side because the benefics -- Jupiter and Venus -- are there, indicating a win for the opposition.

THE DAY AFTER

Another view of this question was given when the contestant himself asked about the same contest on the following day. His question was, "Will I win the Irish Sweepstakes?" The chart was set for June 17, 1961, 34N04 118W15, at 10:05 a.m. Pacific Daylight Time.

Cusps: MC 16 ♉ 11, 11th 20 ♊ 09, 12th 22 ♋ 17, ASC 12 ♌ 19, 2nd 25 ♍ 11, and 3rd 13 ♎ 35.

Planetary positions:

Zodiac	Declination	Zodiac	Declination
☉ 26 ♊ 15	23N23	♄ 28 ♑ 41Rx	20S32
☽ 16 ♌ 12	14N49	♅ 22 ♌ 42	14N37
☿ 10 ♋ 07Rx	21N07	♆ 08 ♏ 50Rx	12S43
♀ 10 ♉ 34	12N16	♀ 05 ♍ 57	21N14
♂ 23 ♌ 25	14N36	MC 16 ♉ 11	16N41
♃ 06 ♎ 20Rx	19S12	ASC 21 ♌ 19	14N24

Analyzing this chart with the horary rules, he is mapped by the first house. Therefore, his rulers are

Uranus, Mars and Pluto (in the house), the Sun (ruling Leo on the house cusp) and the Ascendant. As this is a horary chart, the Moon is his co-ruler.

His honor (tenth house) is governed by Venus (ruler of Taurus on the house cusp) and the Midheaven. Applying aspects, if any, of Venus or the Midheaven with any of those first house rulers will indicate future action as far as this question is concerned.

Let's check them out methodically so as not to miss any possible connection. Venus-Uranus, no aspect. Venus-Mars, none. Venus-Pluto separating trine (past action). Venus-Sun semisquare, as the Sun is moving faster than Venus in this case the aspect is separating. Venus-Ascendant, no aspect. Venus-Moon, separating square.

The Midheaven is applying in a square aspect with Uranus, Mars and the Ascendant. Midheaven-Pluto, no aspect. Midheaven-Sun, semisquare, as the Midheaven is moving faster than the Sun the aspect is separating. Midheaven-Moon, separating square. Because the rulers of his house of honor (Venus and the Midheaven) are not involved in strong, supportive, applying connections to the rulers of the house indicating him (the first), there is no indication that he will win.

Aside from these indications, the ruler of his fifth house of speculation is not in supportive aspect to either of the tenth or first house rulers. He didn't win anything.

If the contest rules are applied to this chart, the strength appears on his side -- seven planets are there. The malefic and benefic planets are split by side. The ruler of each side's honor is located on the opposite side of the wheel. The ruler of the opponents' ability and honor appear on the querent's side. So in this case the horary approach revealed a clearer answer.

Two considerations should be examined. Possibly this question was asked at an improper time and thus resulted in a chart which does not clearly match the ultimate results of the question. The other fact is that if we had applied the cosmodynes to this chart, we may have found that the opponents' side was stronger.

Not much research has been done in this area of sweepstakes and lotteries. However, these simple rules of both approaches can be applied to research further material.

6. OTHER CONTESTS

Trials of strength, of speed, of intellect, of popularity, of memory, or of personal ability may be judged by the contest rules. There are all sorts of situations where one contestant vies for honors even though the conditions do not seem to provide the proper setting for a contest. Among others, those include making the best seller's list, most popular record, movies or video, etc.

Demonstration horoscopes selected for this section include those for winning the Academy of Motion Pictures Oscar Award, dance contests, and the acquisition of medals to show the flexibility of applying the contest rules.

In 1937 Spencer Tracy had won the Oscar for Captain Courageous, and in 1938 he won another Oscar for his acting in Boys' Town. All told, he had been nominated for this honor six times. So in 1962, after he was nominated again for his role in the Judgement at Nuremberg, the question was asked, "Will he win the Oscar?" If he did, it would have been the first time in the Academy's history that best male star was won three times by the same person.

As the contest chart reveals, he did not win the Oscar. You can apply the rules to see this in a chart based on the following data: February 26, 1962, 34N04 118W15, at 6:50 p.m. Pacific Standard Time.

Cusps: MC 21 ♊ 28, 11th 23 ♋ 56, 12th 24 ♌ 33, ASC 22 ♍ 11, 2nd 18 ♎ 49, and 3rd 19 ♏ 04.

Planetary positions:

Zodiac	Declination	Zodiac	Declination
☉ 08 ♓ 02	08S20	♄ 06 ♒ 17	19S05
☽ 01 ♐ 40	15S24	♅ 28 ♌ 04Rx	12N53
☿ 11 ♒ 20	16S59	♆ 13 ♏ 26	14S10
♀ 15 ♓ 28	07S06	♀ 08 ♍ 53Rx	20N42
♂ 19 ♒ 38	15S59	MC 21 ♊ 28	23N10
♃ 23 ♒ 58	14S14	ASC 22 ♍ 11	03N08

Another chart for the same situation but applied to Mary Tyler Moore and her chances of winning an Oscar was set for 1981. Mary had been winning one honor after another for twenty years.

She won three Emmy nominations, two Emmies and had reigned for five years (1961-66) on the Dick Van Dyke Show. She was dubbed the queen of weekly television. In 1965 she received the Foreign Press Golden Globe Award for the best female television personality of the year.

Later she appeared in the Mary Tyler Moore Show and was popular. Television seemed to be her forte. Earlier she had appeared in four motion pictures, but the movie critics had not been as impressed with her talent.

So when she was nominated for an Oscar for her role in the movie Ordinary People, everyone wondered if her luck for receiving honors would continue to hold.

All of this speculation accompanied the mention of another box office celebrity -- Robert Redford. He had directed Ordinary People, and his expertise in this area was lauded by the critics. In fact, he won the Oscar that year for best director. This combination provided solid motivation behind the question: "Will Miss Moore win an Oscar?"

Despite the applause that appeared in print, she did not win the Oscar. This is revealed by the chart erected for February 17, 1981, 34N57 120W26, at 11:09 a.m. Pacific Standard Time.

Cusps: MC 11 ≈ 51, 11th 11 ✶ 13, 12th 19 ♈ 12, ASC 29 ♉ 56, 2nd 25 ♊ 53, and 3rd 18 ♋ 10.

Planetary positions:

Zodiac	Declination	Zodiac	Declination
☉ 29 ≈ 03	11S48	♄ 09 ♎ 01 Rx	01S12
☽ 15 ♌ 16	16N36	♅ 00 ♐ 00	19S56
☿ 28 ≈ 23 Rx	08S30	♆ 24 ♐ 28	22S01
♀ 17 ≈ 10	17S04	♀ 24 ♎ 12	17N27
♂ 08 ✶ 34	09S15	MC 11 ≈ 51	17S15
♃ 09 ♎ 29 Rx	02S18	ASC 29 ♉ 56	20N08

GRAND WALTZ

Warren and Liz Vernon entered the 1957 annual dance contest. They were dubious of winning first place, because they had won it the previous two years. This time the panel of judges was the best in the country at that time: Marge and Gower Champion, Louella Parsons, Betty White, and other television personalities. The Vernons felt that percentage-wise their chances were slim to take the top spot.

These thoughts were running through their minds about three months before the contest was to take place. Suddenly, she had the urge to ask the question; "Will we place in the dance contest?" Even though they both felt that taking top place was doubtful, they wanted to know if they had a chance to come in second or third place. The chart was cast for May 4, 1957, 34N04 118W15, at 4:25 p.m. Pacific Standard time.

Cusps: MC 4♋03, 11th 7♌26, 12th 9♍46, ASC 4♎38, 2nd 2♏05, and 3rd 2♐38.

Planetary positions:

Zodiac	Declination	Zodiac	Declination
☉ 14 ♉ 13	16N06	♄ 13 ♐ 01Rx	20S30
☽ 16 ♋ 19	04S26	♅ 03 ♌ 08	20S03
☿ 15 ♉ 51Rx	17N32	♆ 00 ♍ 54Rx	10S05
♀ 19 ♉ 33	16N48	♇ 27 ♌ 56	22N44
♂ 00 ♋ 13	24N43	MC 04 ♋ 03	23N23
♃ 22 ♍ 10Rx	04N27	ASC 04 ♎ 38	01S52

The east side of the chart represents Warren and Liz, and all of the other contestants -- field against them -- are represented by the west side. Warren and Liz have more planets on their side, as well as the major benefic, Jupiter, and the major malefic, Saturn. The field against them has less planets (strength), plus Venus and Mars on their side.

Venus, ruler of the first house cusp, situated on the other side of the chart, detracts somewhat from Warren and Liz's ability. The Moon, ruler of the Midheaven, is at home in the sign of Cancer in the tenth house, reinforcing their honor. Both the Moon and the Midheaven are trine Neptune in the first house (ability). However, Uranus (in their house of honor) is square Neptune. Balancing these factors, we find some testimony of winning but with certain obstacles in the way of taking the top place.

Although Mars, ruler of the opponent's ability (seventh cusp) is on that side of the chart, Saturn (ruling the opposition's important tenth house cusp -- honor) is located on the couple's side. Angular planets on the east side show more power. Warrent and Liz won second place in the dance contest.

AWARD MEDALS

In many areas contestants strive to win medals. The event most publicized and revered by athletes around the world is at the Olympics where gold (first), silver (second), and bronze (third) medals are awarded the winning contestants in each category. The colorful ceremonies during which these medals are awarded to the winners provide a tremendous emotional experience -- not only for the winners but for the fans as well.

In ceremonies on a smaller and maybe less spectacular scale are those whose medals are awarded to Boy and Girl Scouts, Campfire Girls, 4-H Club members, etc. However, the medals we will concern ourselves with here will be those for the competition in various levels of lessons.

A young woman we will call Sally was enrolled in the dancing classes at the Arthur Murray Dance Studios. A year before she was to be tested, she asked, "Will I win a Silver Medal?" The chart is set for September 20, 1950, 34N04 118W15, at 11:04 a.m. Pacific Standard Time.

Cusps: MC 16 ♍ 43, 11th 16 ♎ 39, 12th 12 ♏ 04, ASC 03 ♐ 52, 2nd 05 ♑ 07, and 3rd 10 ♒ 13.

Planetary positions:

Zodiac	Declination	Zodiac	Declination
☉ 27 ♍ 14	01N06	♄ 23 ♍ 16	04N27
☽ 22 ♑ 06	26S16	♅ 09 ♋ 13	23N25
☿ 20 ♍ 21Rx	01N41	♆ 16 ♎ 22	05S00
♀ 13 ♍ 17	08N06	⚷ 18 ♌ 59	22N52
♂ 26 ♏ 32	20S28	MC 16 ♍ 43	05N14
♃ 29 ♒ 23Rx	12S55	ASC 03 ♐ 52	20S55

-46-

A glance at the chart reveals that Sally will win the silver medal. Two patterns supporting this view jump off the chart to meet the eye. There is more strength on her side -- seven of the ten planets are located there. Her tenth house of honor holds four planets, mapping a strong attraction for a win.

In addition, the planetary rulers of the Ascendant (Jupiter for Sagittarius) and the Midheaven (Mercury for Virgo) are both posited on her side of the wheel, showing further control over the opposing elements. All of the indicators of winning are there except one: That is Venus, a benefic planet, situated on the opposite side.

It was a shoo-in. She did extremely well. One year later, almost to the day (September 11, 1951) at 4:00 p.m., she was awarded the silver medal.

After this, several family crises and setbacks caused her to give up her dance studies for periods of time. She skipped many lessons and became disappointed with her progress. After three years of trying to finish the course, she asked the question, "Will I get the Arthur Murray Dancing Gold Award?" Data: October 30, 1953, 34N04 117W15, at 8:40 p.m. Pacific Daylight Time.

Cusps: MC 10 ♓ 03, 11th 13 ♈ 57, 12th 22 ♉ 39, ASC 28 ♊ 44, 2nd 20 ♋ 26, and 3rd 13 ♌ 03.

Planetary positions:

Zodiac	Declination	Zodiac	Declination
☉ 07 ♍ 28	14S01	♄ 01 ♍ 01	09S43
☽ 25 ♌ 48	10N40	♅ 23 ♋ 07Rx	21N55
☿ 29 ♍ 47	22S57	♆ 24 ♎ 09	07S50
♀ 15 ♎ 34	04S40	♇ 24 ♌ 50	23N18
♂ 29 ♍ 09	01N30	MC 10 ♓ 03	07S48
♃ 26 ♊ 03Rx	22N48	ASC 28 ♊ 44	23N25

Four planets appear on Sally's half of the chart, and we note that there are no planets falling in her important houses of honor (tenth) and ability (first). This whole pattern shows a sign of weakness.

Added to that is the fact that Mercury ruling her Ascendant (ability) and Neptune co-ruling her Midheaven (honor) both appear on the opposite side of the chart from her.

None of these signs are positive indications that she will win a medal. Perhaps even she did not realize that her subconscious mind had gone ahead in time to other things. Such a turn of events is hinted by the twenty-nine degrees rising on the Ascendant. Furthermore, her general attitude and expression, ruled by the third house shows the trend. Both planets therein -- Pluto and the Moon (mentality) -- are square Mercury ruling the Ascendant. These planets fall in fixed signs mapping a certain stubbornness that proved to be an obstacle. In addition, the Mercury involvement shows a scattering of energies rather than concentration.

Outcome: After skipping so many lessons, she gradually lost interest and started to study astrology. Well, we all know how fascinating and tine-consuming this study can become. As a result of her new interest, she never did finish the lessons leading to taking the test for the gold medal.

To close this category of "other contests," we should mention other areas in which these rules can be applied: Tennis matches, such as Wimbledon and the Virginia Slims tournaments, and golf championships like the Bob Hope, Bing Crosby and Dinah Shore tournaments.

7. VARIED TIMES AND LOCATIONS

A quick way to test if a horoscope has been erected properly is to check where the Sun falls in the wheel. The Midheaven (tenth house cusp) represents noon, and the Nadir (fourth house cusp) corresponds to midnight. The Ascendant (first house cusp) falls at sunrise (about 6:00 a.m.), and the Descendant (seventh house cusp) maps sunset (about 6:00 p.m.)

Actually the correspondence of these hours to the chart cusps appears only twice a year. This occurs when the days and nights are equal, at the vernal (March 20/21) and autumnal (September 23/24) equinoxes. The exact correspondence between the chart and time changes with the seasons. In certain areas (latitudes) at different times of year sunrise occurs as early as 3:00 a.m. (Ascendant), and it sets as late as 8:30 p.m. (Descendant). In any case, the Sun's position in the horoscope gives a good indication of the approximate time of birth, whether that is for a person, a question or an idea.

Therefore, if you asked a question about a contest in the a.m. hours, the Sun will be placed on the east side of the chart. Because the fast moving planets (Moon, Mercury, Venus and sometimes others) stay fairly close to the Sun, it is logical to assume that many planets will also be found on the east side in this a.m. chart. If the chart is timed in the p.m. hours, then the west side of the horoscope may be the strongest when measured for strength by the number of planets situated on that side.

In any event, the desire to know who will win a contest must be strong. Then a readable chart will result regardless if the question is asked in the a.m. hours or the p.m. hours.

Some authorities claim that the time span in which the same question can be asked is about twelve hours. That is false. Here Chart C is earlier by thirty days than charts A and B, even though the same question was asked for all three. There are many times with different minds when mental conditions are proper to reflect a horoscope that reveals information about a contest (or even a horary answer). In this chapter we will present horoscopes that demonstrate that principal.

KENNEDY vs NIXON

Here we will discuss three charts for the same political contest. Two of them (Charts A and B) are erected for the same date and place at two different hours. The third chart (Chart C) is set for a different date, place and hour. Data for these charts will be followed by the application of the factors to be considered in judging a political election.

Chart A: August 5, 1960, 34N04 118W15, at 6:40 a.m. Pacific Daylight Time.

Cusps: MC 13 ♉ 23, 11th 17♊33, 12th 19 ♋ 52, ASC 19 ♌02, 2nd 12♍40, and 3rd 10♎51.

Planetary positions:

Zodiac	Declination		Zodiac	Declination
☉ 13 ♌06	18N54		♄ 13 ♑07Rx	22S27
☽ 21♑24	17S30		♅ 20 ♌52	15N11
☿ 23 ♋59	19N42		♆ 06♍28	12S00
♀ 25 ♌13	19N25		♇ 05♍07	20N55
♂ 02 ♊15	19N41		MC 13 ♉ 23	16N51
♃ 24 ♐08Rx	23S07		ASC19 ♌02	15N01

Chart B: August 5, 1960, 34N04 118W15, at 2:07 p.m. Pacific Daylight Time.

Cusps: MC 00 ♍ 52, 11th 02 ♎ 54, 12th 29 ♎ 46, ASC 22 ♏21, 2nd 22 ♐ 20, and 3rd 25♑55.

Planetary positions:

Zodiac	Declination		Zodiac	Declination
☉ 13 ♌25	16N48		♄ 16♑06Rx	22S27
☽ 26♑04	16S46		♅ 20 ♌53	15N11
☿ 24 ♋17	19N43		♆ 06♍28	12S00
♀ 25 ♌26	14N23		♇ 05♍07	20N55
♂ 02 ♊27	19N43		MC 00 ♍52	11N10
♃ 24 ♐07Rx	23S07		ASC22 ♏21	18S24

Chart C: July 6, 1960, 39N48 86W39, at 10:30 a.m. Central Daylight Time.

Cusps: MC 11♊ 58, 11th 15 ♋ 51, 12th 17 ♌03, ASC 14 ♍23, 2nd 09♎11, and 3rd 08♏43.

Planetary positions:

Zodiac	Declination	Zodiac	Declination
☉ 14♋32	22N39	♄ 15♑11Rx	22S11
☽ 13♐31	17S25	♅ 19♌07	15N44
☿ 29♋52Rx	17N01	♆ 06♏24Rx	11S58
♀ 18♋23	23N02	♀ 04♍15	21N19
♂ 11♉43	14N09	MC 11♊58	22N14
♃ 26♐41Rx	23S07	ASC 14♍23	06N09

Chart A: Kennedy is represented by the east side of the chart, and Nixon on the west.

Honor is portrayed by the tenth house. Kennedy's honor rulers are Mars (in the house) and Venus (ruling Taurus on the house cusp). Venus is posited in the first house, signifying that Kennedy has control over his own honor. However, with Mars square Pluto in the first house in Virgo, he would have a tendency to talk too much, perhaps in circles and to be too fussy and persnickety about some subjects. This could affect his reputation and drawing power in certain circles of society.

Nixon's map is another story. His honor (fourth house) is weak because no planets energize the house by being stationed there. Furthermore, both rulers of Scorpio on the house cusp (Pluto and Mars) are square each other showing obstacles. As they appear in Kennedy's first and tenth house, these planets symbolize the fact that Kennedy has control over Nixon's honor.

Personal ability is pictured by the first house, Kennedy's prowess is ruled by Uranus, Venus, and Pluto (in the house) and by the Sun (ruling the house cusp). He would be inclined to grandstand (Leo) and to be somewhat pushy (Mars square Pluto) with his personality. Still, all of these rulers are located on his own side of the wheel.

Nixon's personal ability (the seventh house) is weak. No planets occupy the house to energize it. The planetary co-rulers of Aquarius on the house cusp are split by sides. Uranus, one of those rulers, falls in Kennedy's first house, signifying that Kennedy has some control over Nixon's personal ability.

As for the luck factor, the placement of the benefics and the malefics comes out even, neither favoring nor detracting from either nominee's race.

Kennedy's side also shows more power and strength because seven of the ten planets are posited on his side of the horoscope.

Chart B: Kennedy is represented by the east side of the wheel and Nixon by the west.

Kennedy's honor (tenth house) holds Pluto, ruler of his Ascendant. Mercury, governing Virgo on the Midheaven, appears on the other side of the chart. This Mercury position shows that Nixon has some control, but with Mercury trine the Ascendant (Kennedy's ability), some support is also indicated for Kennedy.

Nixon's honor (fourth house) is weak. There are no planets there. Pisces on the cusp means that Neptune and Jupiter are rulers of his honor. Because both of these planets appear on the other side of the wheel, Nixon has little control over his own honor.

Kennedy's personal ability (first house) also reflects a bit of ambivalence. The co-rulers of Scorpio, Pluto and Mars, are split by sides. Even so, as Pluto is located in the tenth house, Kennedy has control over his own ability to a certain extent.

Nixon's house of personal ability (seventh) holds Mars. This would take something away from Kennedy's ability (because Mars is a co-ruler of Scorpio rising). Venus, co-ruler of that seventh house is placed on Nixon's side. These patterns map a closeness as far as ability is concerned, even though Nixon's is a little stronger.

As for the luck factor, we find the same situation as displayed in Chart A. Even-sided benefics and malefics neither favor nor block the nominee's progress.

Analyzing the side count of the planets as far as the strength goes, the distribution here is even -- five on either side. However, Kennedy has a slight edge. His ability, Pluto, is located in his own tenth house of honor. Another configuration signifying strength in both of Kennedy's important houses is the exact parallel aspect of Mercury (tenth house) and Mars (first house).

Chart C: We allot Kennedy to the east side of this horoscope and Nixon to the west.

Kennedy's honor (tenth house) is ruled by the Sun (in the house) and Mercury (ruler of Gemini on the house cusp). Notice that this Sun closely opposes Saturn, mapping a tendency to attract restriction and a negative response. As Saturn is on the opposing side, there is an indication of the opponent to hold down the enthusiasm stirred up by Kennedy.

Nixon's honor (fourth house) is much stronger than Kennedy's. Energy comes from the Moon, Jupiter and Saturn actually located in the house. That Sun-Saturn opposition indicates restriction for Nixon as it did for Kennedy. The stimulation of such a separative complex is intimately tied in with the reputations of both men.

Kennedy's ability (first house) is also ruled by Mercury (as is his Midheaven). With Mercury situated in the eleventh house, friends and well-wishers will play an important role in his progress. They have an impact on both his honor and his ability.

A double rulership sign appears on the cusp of Nixon's house of ability (the seventh). Pisces there is ruled by Neptune and Jupiter. Jupiter occupies his house of honor (the fourth), but Neptune is located on the other side of the chart.

Analyzing the luck factor, we find Jupiter on Nixon's side and Venus on Kennedy's. Thus, neither side is emphasized. However, both malefics (Saturn and Mars) appear on Nixon's side, indicating some discord.

These factors describe a close race when taken together and balanced against each other. Kennedy had control over his honor and ability (Mercury). Nixon had control over his honor (Jupiter) but not complete control over his ability (Uranus and Saturn).

Kennedy's side pictures more strength (six planets there). That strength had enough attractive power to override Nixon's strong tenth house (the fourth here) allowed Kennedy to win the election.

In all three charts there is no crystal clear tabulation of factors to indicate total strength and luck for a particular side to win. They all map a crossover of control. That signifies a close struggle to attain success. In spite of that, in each case there is a bit more testimony for the east side of the wheel.

History tells us that John F. Kennedy won the presidential election in 1960. These charts picture the close popular vote. Kennedy received only 166,399 more popular votes than Nixon did.

TIMING

Looking at these three charts from the time angle demonstrates the opening idea of this chapter. The Sun's position in a wheel should approximate the local mean time for which the chart is calculated. Chart A was set for 5:47 a.m. Local Mean Time, which is after sunrise in August at 34N04 latitude. There the Sun appears in the twelfth house which represents approximately 6:00 to 8:00 a.m. on the clock.

Chart B is erected for 1:14 p.m. Local Mean Time on the same day. The Sun appears in the ninth house, which in a general way stands for a time span from noon until 2:00 p.m. This Sun position is 7 hours and 27 minutes ahead of Chart A's Sun.

Chart C shows another hour -- 9:43:14 a.m. Local Mean Time. This would lead one to believe that the Sun should fall in the eleventh house which represents approximately 8:00 to 10:00 a.m. on the clock.

The key word here is approximately. Due to seasonal changes and the north/south swing of the planets in declination, the Sun will often appear in the next or previous house. In those cases it is usually located not far from the house cusp, especially as related to the tenth and fourth house cusps. The Ascendant and Descendant relationship has a wider variation. An understanding of this relationship of time to the chart makes it easy to test the Sun's position against the clock time for proper chart calculation.

Along this line of thought we should note that all of the planets travel at varying rates of ununiform motion. Therefore, every so often we see strong clusters of planets occupying a sign or two in the zodiac. At these times when the Sun, Mercury and Venus are moving through the same section of the zodiac in which several planets occupy at the time, the cluster (or stellium) may appear on one side of the contest chart. This symbolizes a great deal of strength for the contestant that is pictured by that side of the horoscope.

MAYOR'S RACE

Another instance of the same question being asked at two different locations and hours twelve days apart was a mayoral race held in 1969. Samuel Yorty and Tom Bradley were opposing each other on the ticket to elect a mayor of the City of Los Angeles. "Will Yorty win the Mayor's race?" was asked for both Chart D and Chart E.

Chart D: May 14, 1969, 34N04 118W15, at 8:12 p.m. Pacific Daylight Time.

Cusps: MC 10 ♍ 57, 11th 12 ♎ 19, 12th 08 ♏ 12, ASC 00 ♐ 11, 2nd 00 ♑ 58, and 3rd 05 ♒ 36.

Planetary positions:

Zodiac	Declination		Zodiac	Declination
☉ 24 ♉ 07	18N48		♄ 01 ♉ 53	10N01
☽ 10 ♉ 16	18N05		♅ 00 ♎ 06Rx	00N39
☿ 11 ♊ 44	23N53		♆ 27 ♏ 26Rx	17S52
♀ 14 ♉ 36	05N42		♀ 22 ♍ 30Rx	17N25
♂ 14 ♐ 49Rx	23S40		MC 10 ♍ 57	07N28
♃ 26 ♍ 13Rx	02N51		ASC 00 ♐ 11	20S12

Chart E: May 26, 1969, 34N25 119W42, at 7:00 p.m. Pacific Daylight Time.

Cusps: MC 03 ♍ 00, 11th 04 ♎ 43, 12th 01 ♏ 21, ASC 23 ♏ 43, 2nd 23 ♐ 52, and 3rd 02 ♑ 41.

Planetary positions:

Zodiac	Declination		Zodiac	Declination
☉ 05 ♊ 37	21N15		♄ 03 ♉ 18	10N29
☽ 05 ♎ 58	03S02		♅ 29 ♍ 55Rx	00N43
☿ 09 ♊ 08Rx	20N29		♆ 27 ♏ 07Rx	17S48
♀ 22 ♈ 02	07N09		♀ 22 ♍ 25Rx	17N22
♂ 11 ♐ 31Rx	23S55		MC 03 ♍ 00	10N29
♃ 26 ♍ 28	02N50		ASC 23 ♏ 43	18S43

Chart D: Yorty is mapped by the east side of the figure and Bradley by the west side.

Yorty's honor house holds Pluto, Jupiter and Uranus. Mercury should also be considered a ruler as it governs Virgo on the tenth house cusp. Even though Mercury is situated on the other side of the chart, this tenth house should be considered strong as it is energized by three planets.

Bradley shows no planets in his honor house (the fourth). Also, the co-rulers of this house (Neptune and Jupiter for Pisces on the house cusp) both appear on the opposite side of the wheel. Jupiter falling in Yorty's tenth house shows a potential for him to control Bradley's honor.

Yorty's personal ability (first house) is ruled by Mars (located in the house) and Jupiter (for Sagittarius on the house cusp). Mars opposes Mercury which could indicate loose lips to the point of self-detriment. However, that aspect is separating from its perfect position symbolizing that the potential is in the past. Jupiter in the tenth house signifies Yorty's control over his own honor and reputation.

Bradley's personal ability (seventh house) is ruled by Mercury, which also governs the seventh house cusp. Notice, that viewed from this side of the chart, Mercury is applying to the opposition of Mars, hinting that the grapevine could pick up on the statements he makes and very easily twist them to make him look less attractive as a candidate.

Luck: The benefics and malefics are split by side location and cancel each other out.

Even though there are five planets in each half of the wheel, Yorty's vital tenth and first houses are stronger than Bradley's. Such additional power indicates that Yorty had a good chance of winning the election. He did.

Chart E: Yorty is represented by the east side and Bradley by the west.

In this chart Yorty's honor (tenth house) is ruled by Pluto, Jupiter and Uranus (posited in the house) and by Mercury (ruling Virgo on the house cusp). This gives a strong house of honor for Yorty even though Mercury is located in Bradley's first house (the seventh).

Bradley's honor (fourth house) is weaker due to the fact that there are no planets occupying the house. The rulers of Pisces on the cusp -- Neptune and Jupiter -- are located on Yorty's side. In addition, their position is highly significant, because they are situated in Yorty's vital tenth and first houses, giving him the upper hand.

Yorty's personal ability and technique (first house) is also energized. Neptune and Mercury occupy the house. Adding to this is Pluto (governing Scorpio rising) co-ruler of his prowess and is located in his tenth house strengthening his power to control his honor and ability.

There are three planetary rulers of Bradley's personal ability house (seventh). The Sun and Mercury (in the house) and Venus (governing the sign of Taurus on the house cusp). All three planets are posited on his side of the chart. Mars receives an applying opposition aspect from the Sun and Mercury, mapping difficulties and obstacles for him to overcome.

The luck factor does not map help or hindrance because the benefics and malefics are split by side.

Overall we see that Yorty is in control of himself and his honor. Bradley has no control over his honor, and to express his personal ability effectively he would have to overcome some resistance and barriers. Another plus factor for Yorty is the strength factor, represented by the six planets occupying his half of the wheel. So it is not surprising to learn that Yorty won the election.

When the tally of the delineation measures for each side is close, then the calculations of the cosmodynes usually reveal a sharper picture of the power and luck of a contestant, as well as where those factors are centered.

Especially important in gauging the power are the parallel aspects, including those to the Midheaven and Ascendant. Parallels intensify the potential symbolized in relation to the entire horoscope.

For instance, look back at the delineations listed for Chart C. There are several declinations falling at twenty-two and twenty-three degrees, meaning that several parallel aspects are formed because we allow an orb of one degree. These parallels add to the power of certain areas in the chart mapped by those planetary positions.

We will discuss the cosmodynes in the next chapter.

8. ROLE OF PROGRESSIONS AND COSMODYNES

In most of these contest charts we have been asking if a single person will be the winner. In others, we asked about a team winning. Regardless of whether they compete as a single entrant or as a team, all contestants have natal charts which are of prime significance when one attempts to delineate what to expect in their lives at any given time. The question "what" is of utmost importance, because it has a bearing on general trends which fashion the environment.

Natal charts, either of a person or of a team, can be progressed so as to judge if there is sufficient power and luck to attract a win. By progressions we refer to three post-natal releases of energy. (1) Major progressions are signified by a day for a year after birth in the ephemeris; (2) minor progressions are mapped by approximately a month for a year in the ephemeris after birth; and (3) transit progressions (commonly referred to simply as transits) are represented by a day for a day after birth in the ephemeris -- the current zodiacal positions on any date.

The Midheaven and the Ascendant are progressed and with the ten progressed planets, they are placed around the outside of the natal wheel. That natal wheel is the strongest and basic potential indicator. The progressions merely point out the times when various areas of the natal chart will be stimulated to the point of attractive strength matching the environment.

The Midheaven is progressed at the same rate as the progressed Sun (solar arc). In other words, the span of degrees between the progressed Sun and the progressed Midheaven is always the same as that distance between the natal Sun and the natal Midheaven. Then the progressed Ascendant is calculated for the birth latitude from the position of the progressed Midheaven.

The minor progressed Midheaven and the minor progressed Ascendant are handled in the same manner for the birth latitude. However, when the same rules are applied for figuring transit Ascendant, the latitude of the place where the event takes place (not the birth latitude) is used.

Remember that even though the tenth house in a contest chart may show a great deal of stimulation, one does not win a contest unless the tenth house of his own natal chart (or the team chart, if a team is playing) is strongly energized by progressions at the time of a the contest.

Expressed in other words, we can say that the natal chart with its progressions holds more weight than a contest chart alone. Furthermore, if a contest chart covers a long span of time before the results are announced, it too can be progressed to see which areas are stimulated. These areas of the horoscope will picture the events and conditions associated with the contest -- those that assume importance from time to time.

Natal charts present potentials only. They do not promise or deny anything. What the native does with the energy released by progressions can be and should be counseled through the use of balancing the progressed positions against the natal positions. They always indicate the "stop" and "go" signals for action.

Each house in the wheel governs a certain department in the life of the native. Unless there are progressions activating a planetary ruler of a house, the affairs ruled by that house will not be prominent enough to affect the native's life.

Progressed aspects can be of any nature to stir up action in a specific department of life. By that is meant that squares, oppositions and other discordant aspects do not deny a happy conclusion to a project ruled by that area in the life (house). Nor do trines, sextiles and other harmonious aspects stimulate the birth chart in such a way as to always promise success. How these progressed aspects energize the natal chart for potential events is more important than their classification as positive or negative.

For instance, a person may have a harmonious tenth house natally, and by progression a couple of oppositions form to the rulers of that house. What this indicates is that some obstacles may present themselves but the basic harmony of the birth chart will portray a situation that describes a person who with intelligent effort can overcome these obstacles. Or, even a person who will be able to turn these obstacles into stepping stones to success. On the other hand, if no progressions stimulate the natal tenth house, the person will not win a contest.

An example of this necessary energy release in relation to event can be seen when a progressed aspect stimulates an appropriate house. In Chapter 6, Warren and Liz asked if they would win the dance contest. Even though they are partners, she posted the question herself. Therefore, progressions in her natal chart involving the tenth house of winning would be of first rank.

At the time they won the contest, her natal tenth house was activated. Her major progressed Mars was in trine aspect with the natal Sun in her tenth house, mapping an opportunity and luck for her to win. Warren's birth hour was unknown, so his current progressions were unavailable. But this win would be a splendid event, the dance contest, for testing a rectified chart. Because for him to attract such an event into his life, his horoscope would have to map active tenth house stimulation. There is no doubt he had a major progression operating even though we do not know what it was.

PRECISE CONTEST RESEARCH

In order to zero in precisely on the amount of attractive power and luck of a contestant's chances of winning, cosmodyne measurements can be applied. This technique, which is a simple mathematical yardstick[1], resulting in a certain percentage within one frame of reference -- one chart, can be applied to both natal and progressed elements.

After the components are determined by a percentage of power, harmony and/or discord in the natal chart, then one-half of the natal power, harmony or discord is allotted to the major progressed planets, Midheaven and Ascendant. This procedure is clearly described and illustrated in *The Astrodyne Manual,* by Elbert Benjamine[2].

To prevent a misunderstanding of the terms used in this technique, we should make it clear that cosmodynes (sometimes termed astrodynes) are defined as expressing three types of measurement. (1) Astrodynes (units of astrological power) refer to the power or strength of a chart element -- planet, sign, house, aspect. (2) Harmodynes refer to supportive or harmonious indications. (3) Discordynes refer to restrictive or discordant potentials.

In 1948 and 1949 the Church of Light Research Department erected and studied one hundred contest charts of football games. All of the charts were erected at hours and dates before the games were played. A favorite team was selected, and the question asked was, "Will the favorite team win the game?"

Every aspect involving the planet in the tenth house, those ruling the cusp of the tenth house, those ruling an intercepted sign in the tenth house, is any, and those of the Midheaven, were considered in this test. Each of these is considered a ruler of the tenth house in a chart. For this research study a short-cut method was used to test the outcomes of the game against the individual charts. The cosmodynes of all of the harmonious aspects were tallied. Then the cosmodynes of all of the discordant aspects were totaled.

If there were more harmodynes than discordynes represented by the tenth house, the team asked about was judged to win the contest. If the total discordynes was higher, it was judged that the team asked about would lose the game. This rule proved to be correct in 100 percent of the cases.

The results of this interesting research can be found in *Astrology: Thirty Years Research* [3] by Doris Chase Doane. The following table is taken from that work.

JUDGING CONTEST WINNERS

Chart to select a winning football team............................100
Charts for winner of event judged correctly.......................75
Charts for tenth house predominatly harmonius................75
Charts with loser of event judged correctly.......................25
Charts with tenth house predominatly discordant............25

Of course, it goes without saying that general approach was less precise than a complete report of cosmodynes on each individual chart. But in those days computers were not available as they are today to do the multiple calculations demanded by this technique. Nevertheless, the general approach shows the weight of the tenth house to be an indication of winning.

SUSTAINING POWER

How progressions and cosmodynes can picture the events in life are graphically shown in the horoscopes of two prominent Olympic athletes: Mark Andrew Spitz and Bruce Jenner. Not only their wins were shown by the activity of progressions to their natal charts, so were their life directions after the Olympics in which they participated became history.

Mark Andrew Spitz was born February 10, 1950, in Modesto, California, 37N39 121W00, at 5:45 p.m. Pacific Standard Time. Data is from his birth certificate as given to me by John E. Daniel.

In the 1972 Olympic Games held in Munich, West Germany, Spitz emerged as the world's premier swimmer by winning an unprecedented seven gold medals between August 28 and September 4, 1972.

How the astrological potential was energized at that time was shown by the major progressions. One day in the middle of this time span was selected for the progressions, September 1, 1972. They appear on the outside wheel of his natal chart.

In order to check out this stimulation, we need to recall that honor and recognition are governed by the tenth house, and that the Sun corresponds to whether or not the native will stand out from the crowd in some way.

Spitz's tenth house of honor is solely ruled by Venus, because Taurus occupies the Midheaven and there are no other planets in the house. Venus is located in Aquarius in the sixth house. Venus is not active in his natal chart. It is involved with only three aspects: Sextile the Moon, trine Mars, and sesquisquare Saturn. A glance at Spitz's Cosmodyne Report reveals that Venus, with 3.5% of the total chart power, is the second weakest point in his horoscope.

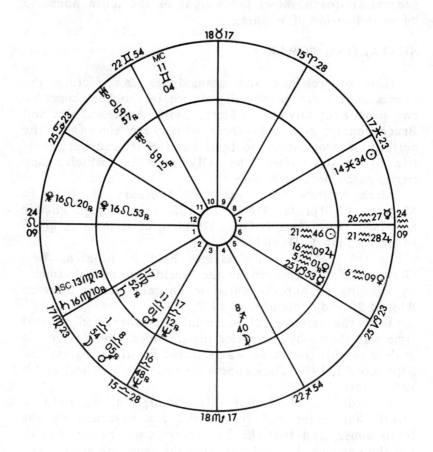

Natal Chart for Mark Andrew Spitz
February 10, 1950   5:45 PM PST
Modesto, California   37 N 29   121 W 00

POWER		HARMONY		DISCORD	
M.C.	62.87 - 14.7%	NEPTUNE	15.30 - 30.8%		
PLUTO	58.10 - 13.6	JUPITER	9.89 - 19.9		
JUPITER	47.55 - 11.1	MOON	6.26 - 12.6		
ASC.	44.57 - 10.4	VENUS	6.13 - 12.3		
SUN	40.26 - 9.4	SATURN	5.46 - 11.0		
MOON	33.71 - 7.9	MERCURY	3.60 - 7.3		
URANUS	31.50 - 7.4	MARS	3.06 - 6.2		
NEPTUNE	28.16 - 6.6			URANUS	3.29 - 4.9%
MARS	25.69 - 6.0			PLUTO	8.65 - 13.0
SATURN	25.36 - 5.9			M.C.	17.03 - 25.5
VENUS	15.04 - 3.5			SUN	18.11 - 27.2
MERCURY	14.42 - 3.4			ASC.	19.60 - 29.4

POWER		HARMONY		DISCORD	
LEO	122.80 - 20.6%	LIBRA	21.42 - 38.4%		
AQUARIUS	117.06 - 19.6	SAGITTARIUS	11.21 - 20.1		
TAURUS	70.38 - 11.8	VIRGO	7.26 - 13.0		
LIBRA	61.37 - 10.3	CAPRICORN	6.33 - 11.4		
SAGITTARIUS	57.49 - 9.7	PISCES	6.30 - 11.3		
CANCER	48.36 - 8.1	GEMINI	1.80 - 3.3		
VIRGO	32.57 - 5.5	ARIES	1.53 - 2.8		
CAPRICORN	27.10 - 4.6			CANCER	.15 - 0.3%
SCORPIO	20.95 - 3.5			SCORPIO	1.40 - 2.6
PISCES	18.93 - 3.2			AQUARIUS	1.54 - 2.9
ARIES	12.84 - 2.2			TAURUS	13.96 - 25.7
GEMINI	7.21 - 1.2			LEO	37.30 - 68.7

POWER		HARMONY		DISCORD	
SIXTH	129.95 - 21.8%	THIRD	18.37 - 36.0%		
TWELFTH	74.96 - 12.6	SECOND	10.32 - 20.2		
TENTH	70.38 - 11.8	EIGHTH	6.30 - 12.4		
FIRST	64.70 - 10.9	FIFTH	4.95 - 9.7		
SECOND	58.26 - 9.8	FOURTH	4.87 - 9.6		
FOURTH	54.66 - 9.2	SIXTH	4.25 - 8.4		
ELEVENTH	38.71 - 6.5	NINTH	1.53 - 3.0		
THIRD	35.68 - 6.0	SEVENTH	.54 - 1.1		
FIFTH	23.77 - 4.0			ELEVENTH	1.48 - 3.0%
EIGHTH	18.93 - 3.2			TWELFTH	5.52 - 11.2
SEVENTH	14.22 - 2.4			TENTH	13.96 - 28.2
NINTH	12.84 - 2.2			FIRST	28.66 - 57.8

Aspects of the natal Midheaven include squares to the Sun, Jupiter and Pluto; trines with Mercury and Saturn; a semisquare to Uranus; and an inconjunct with Neptune. His Midheaven power totals up to be the strongest point (14.7%) in his chart according to the cosmodyne report. The combination of the Venus and Midheaven cosmodynes put the tenth house in the third place (11.8%) as far as power goes.

These configurations signify a potential for prominence when activated. How the birth chart potential was energized enough to attract honor and recognition at this time is mapped by major progressions stimulating this area of his horoscope.

As his progressed chart shows, in 1972 his major progressed Jupiter had closed the conjunction to the Sun within the one degree orb demanded for progressed aspects. At the same time the major progressed Midheaven was stationed at eleven degrees of Gemini, just passing (by three minutes) an exact trine with natal Mars in Libra from the tenth house.

In addition to those indications for attracting honor, rallying forces formed in the chart to coincide with the direction of his energies. They are mapped especially by planets occupying sixteen or seventeen degrees of a sign in both the natal and the progressed positions.

Spitz's minor progressed positions on August 28, 1972:

☉ 5≏48	♂ 09♍10	♆ 19≏31
☽ 1♊41	♃ 06♈58Rx	♀ 21♌16
☿ 00♏10	♄ 08≏00	MC 22♒19
♀ 12♍10	♅ 14♋00	ASC 16♊16

Whenever a major event occurs in life, research reveals that the native's chart shows at least one major progression operating within one degree of the perfect aspect. This progressed aspect involves planetary rulers of the horoscope houses governing the environment of that event as we described above. But in addition, there is also at least one minor progression involving either a major or natal position that reinforces the major progression mapping the event. The minors are not considered in aspect with each other.

In Mark's chart at the time he won the gold medals Venus or the Midheaven would have to be activated and reinforced with energy represented by minor progressions, because they are the rulers of his tenth house.

If these minors are placed around the outside of the chart, it will be easy to see that minor progressed Jupiter is sextile major progressed Venus. Minor progressed Midheaven is conjunction the natal Sun and major progressed Jupiter. Aside from that last aspect mentioned above, the natal Sun (significance) is receiving a trine aspect from minor progressed Moon. Minor Sun is also square natal Mercury.

Reinforcement energy was also indicated by the minor Ascendant, at sixteen degrees of Gemini, energizing the basic, natal and progressed rallying forces in the chart. However, all of this is quite mild as far as added power and energy goes compared to that formed in Jenner's chart as we shall see.

Spitz's transiting progressed positions on September 1, 1972, at Munich, West Germany (48N09).

⊙ 08 ♍39   ♂ 10♍57   ♆ 02 ♐ 34
☽ 14 ♊ 46   ♃ 28 ♐ 33   ♀ 01 ♎ 01
☿ 22 ♌ 22   ♄ 19 ♊ 42   MC 05 ♑ 10
♀ 22 ♋ 54   ♅ 16 ♎ 19   ASC 11 ♈ 38

Important events come into the life when the natal chart is energized by a major progression and reinforced by a minor progression. But nothing ever happens, occurs or manifests until a transit progression ties in with either an appropriate natal position or major progressed position (not minor) embraced in the event pattern.

Place these transit progressions around the outside of Mark's wheel. The minor progressed Midheaven is semisextile natal and major progressed Venus at the time of his wins. The transit progressed Mercury is opposing his natal Sun. Transit Uranus, at 16 degrees of Libra, is triggering the rallying forces in the chart.

These stimulators certainly indicated that Spitz could come before the public. Yet there is not enough activity in the chart to keep him at the peak of attention for any length of time. Sustaining power associated with his tenth house is not strong enough.

Bruce Jenner was born on October 28, 1949, in Mount Kisco, New York, 41N12 73W44, at 6:00 a.m. Eastern Standard Time. At a dinner honoring Olympic Champions held by the San Francisco Press Club, I obtained this data directly from Jenner.

At the July 1976 XXI Olympiad Games in Montreal, Canada, he scored an unusual record of 8,618 points in the decathlon. This event includes ten running, throwing, and jumping competitions. The decathlon is rated the most difficult of all athletic competition, because it is the most demanding of the contestant's strength, endurance, speed and skill (see Figure 32).

How did this situation correspond with the activity in his horoscope? The major progressions for August 1, 1976 appear in the outside wheel of the chart.

When an aspect forming in the natal chart is within one degree of the perfect aspect, it represents strong urges within the native that demand expression, insist upon attention and seek prominence. Such planets within a one-degree orb of aspect form a progression at birth.

In Jenner's chart, the natal Sun (recognition) is located in the first house of personal interest, and it is within one degree of a trine with Uranus. All of his life so far this pattern has been operating as a major progression, because Uranus travels slowly by progression. The Sun being placed in the fixed sign of Scorpio indicates a strong and self-driven perseverance, the sticking-with-it required of an outstanding athlete. This is a quality that Bruce was born with and one he has developed in an active way through his formative years while this long time aspect was within orb of a trine.

These traits are also associated with his physical body, because the Sun appears in the first house. The Sun is involved in ten aspects: Square the Moon, Jupiter and the Midheaven; conjunction Mercury and the Ascendant; sextile Mars; semisquare Venus and Saturn; parallel Mars; and trine Uranus. According to Jenner's Cosmodyne Report, the Sun represents the most power in the chart (15.8%).

Jenner's natal tenth house is stimulated by aspects of Pluto, Mars and the Midheaven in addition to the strong Sun, ruling Leo on the house cusp. Pluto hooks into six aspects, Mars to eight, and the Midheaven into seven and the Sun with Ten. These aspects all contribute to the

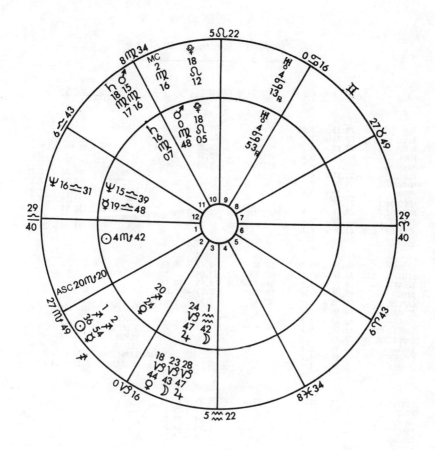

Natal Chart for Bruce Jenner
October 28, 1949   6:00 AM EST
Mount Kisco, New York   41 N 12   73 W 44

POWER		HARMONY		DISCORD	
SUN	79.13 - 15.8%	PLUTO	24.77 - 31.6%		
ASC.	58.71 - 11.8	URANUS	23.11 - 29.5		
M.C.	48.63 - 9.7	MERCURY	14.26 - 18.2		
MOON	42.76 - 8.6	VENUS	10.34 - 13.2		
MARS	42.67 - 8.5	NEPTUNE	5.83 - 7.4		
PLUTO	39.71 - 8.0			MARS	.26 - 0.3%
URANUS	38.85 - 7.8			JUPITER	6.78 - 7.3
VENUS	36.71 - 7.4			ASC.	10.99 - 11.8
MERCURY	32.66 - 6.5			SUN	11.18 - 12.0
NEPTUNE	28.06 - 5.6			SATURN	12.54 - 13.5
SATURN	28.03 - 5.6			MOON	24.13 - 26.0
JUPITER	23.38 - 4.7			M.C.	27.00 - 29.1

POWER		HARMONY		DISCORD	
LIBRA	156.14 - 20.7%	LIBRA	19.43 - 40.6%		
LEO	127.90 - 17.0	CANCER	11.04 - 23.1		
SCORPIO	99.72 - 13.3	SAGITTARIUS	8.64 - 18.1		
VIRGO	87.04 - 11.6	TAURUS	5.17 - 10.8		
CANCER	60.23 - 8.0	GEMINI	3.56 - 7.4		
AQUARIUS	59.48 - 7.9			PISCES	.24 - 0.4%
ARIES	42.67 - 5.7			ARIES	.26 - 0.5
SAGITTARIUS	42.55 - 5.7			SCORPIO	5.05 - 9.4
CAPRICORN	37.39 - 5.0			VIRGO	5.68 - 10.6
TAURUS	18.35 - 2.4			LEO	7.82 - 14.6
PISCES	12.86 - 1.7			CAPRICORN	13.05 - 24.4
GEMINI	8.17 - 1.1			AQUARIUS	21.49 - 40.1

POWER		HARMONY		DISCORD	
TENTH	170.57 - 22.7%	TWELFTH	25.25 - 40.4%		
FIRST	156.19 - 20.8	SECOND	14.77 - 23.7		
THIRD	80.15 - 10.7	NINTH	11.04 - 17.7		
TWELFTH	79.08 - 10.5	EIGHTH	8.73 - 14.0		
SECOND	63.14 - 8.4	FOURTH	2.64 - 4.2		
NINTH	60.23 - 8.0			SIXTH	.13 - 0.2%
ELEVENTH	44.36 - 5.9			SEVENTH	.13 - 0.2
EIGHTH	26.52 - 3.5			FIFTH	.24 - 0.4
SIXTH	21.34 - 2.8			ELEVENTH	5.42 - 7.9
SEVENTH	21.34 - 2.8			TENTH	8.08 - 11.9
FOURTH	16.72 - 2.2			FIRST	17.00 - 24.9
FIFTH	12.86 - 1.7			THIRD	37.18 - 54.5

power (22.7%) represented by his tenth house -- the strongest house in the chart.

At the time of the Montreal Games, Jenner had a great many major progressions activating his Sun and the tenth house. Aside from the Uranus contact mentioned above, his major progressed Sun was sextile the natal Moon, square the major progressed Midheaven, square the natal Mars, and semisquare Neptune.

Tenth house activity was mapped by the major progressed Sun aspects cited above, as well as others. Major progressed Mars (tenth house ruler) was semisextile natal Neptune and conjunction natal Saturn. Major progressed Pluto (a tenth house ruler) was semisextile major progressed Saturn and inconjunct major progressed Venus. From these we see that Jenner had much more major chart stimulation at the time of his win than Spitz did

Jenner's minor progressed positions on August 1, 1976:

☉ 06♏15	♂ 15♍19	♆ 19≏54
☽ 06♏00	♃ 05♈49Rx	♇ 04♌24
☿ 16♏51	♄ 09≏14	MC 06♌55
♀ 20♍31	♅ 13♋57Rx	ASC 00♏55

In Jenner's horoscope Pluto, Mars, and the Midheaven or the Sun (tenth house rulers) would be reinforced at this time by minor progressions. The minor Sun is square the natal Midheaven. Minor Pluto is conjunction the natal Midheaven. Also the minor Pluto is square the natal Sun and semisextile natal Uranus, energizing the natal Sun-Uranus trine. Minor Mars is conjunction the natal Saturn and the major progressed Mars. Minor Ascendant is sextile natal Mars. In addition there are other aspects providing reinforcement for activating the rallying forces in the chart areas involved (see Figure 35).

Jenner's transit positions for August 1, 1976 at Montreal (45N32):

☉ 09♌50	♂ 15♍58	♆ 11♐19Rx
☽ 27≏41	♃ 22♉33	♇ 09≏27
☿ 27♌08	♄ 07♌00	MC 10♉30
♀ 22♌11	♅ 03♏14	ASC 21♌01

The transit progressions triggering the chart patterns symbolizing his honor, recognition and popularity rulers included Mars conjunction natal Saturn and major progressed Mars. Transit progressed Jupiter was in orb of a trine aspect with his natal Moon, which stimulated the natal inconjunct aspect formed between the Moon and Mars.

Long-lasting natal progressions show a sustaining power in Jenner's horoscope. This coincided with his success in achieving goals that he began to develop and cultivate when he was preparing for his win at the Olympics.

THE AFTERMATH

After Spitz won the gold medals, the "Mark Spitz look" became the rage. Male models started to become look-a-likes of his modish hairstyle hanging just slightly over the ears and his well-trimmed mustache. He was in demand by every media.

He jumped at the first Hollywood agency offer and went the rounds of the television talk shows (at which he was not very fluent and appeared wooden), did television and media ads for sports clothes and shoes -- the regular route of a celebrity in demand.

This total exposure was the result of poor marketing. Soon criticism was heaped upon him and his efforts, and he turned into an intense and gray-looking "I know it all" type. The public turned away from him and he fell from favor. His fall was so drastic and complete that one male model of the day who had the "Mark Spitz look" down to the last eyebrow was let go from his contract through no fault of his own, other than his appearance.

Mark's seventh gold medal was won on September 4, 1972. By this time Arab terrorists had stirred up a feud with the Israel athletes. The age-old antagonism between the Jews and the Arabs was brewing and about to burst into flame right there in the Olympic Village, even though the place was guarded. On September 5, the next early morning at 4:20 a.m. the killings started. When it was all over, seventeen people had been killed.

The morning after the murders, an audience of 80,000 filed into the Olympic Stadium for a hastily arranged memorial service. But Spitz did not attend. He had fled the country, because he was a Jew and feared for his life. A few days after he returned home, he was signed to a show business contract for theatrical enterprises.

That terrorist event and the poor reputation he gained at the Olympics for girl chasing darkened his victory. His natal T-square from the twelfth house of disappointments (Pluto), to the third of his state of mind (Neptune), to the sixth house of his general health (Jupiter) described the conditions. Neptune also rules the eighth house of death because Pisces occupies the house cusp. An afflicted Pluto maps insidious forces working behind the scenes. He literally fled for his life after being smuggled (twelfth house) out of the athletes' quarters.

As with all humans both of these athletes had their ups and downs. But Jenner seemed to have more control over his development. After the win at Montreal, he was approached by a Hollywood agency. However, he did not sign up for anything and everything right away. He scrutinized every offer carefully. "It [Olympic exposure] can get you in the door" he said, "but to stay inside you have to deliver."

He has certainly delivered. From just two days of athletic achievement, he has applied his personal and physical assets in such a way as to become a success in many areas. He is still active in sports. In fact, he is noted for being an all-'round athlete. He has become a sportscaster, champion auto racer, a television and movie actor, a lecturer in great demand, to name but a few of his achievements.

Jenner's dark moments came from marital stress. His wife had been his greatest supporter while he trained for the Olympics. But soon after their goal was achieved, their marriage began to disintegrate. Eventually they divorced. Jenner's marriage house (the seventh) is ruled exclusively by Mars because Aries appears on the house cusp and no other planets occupy the house. Natally, Mars is sesquisquare (agitation) Venus, and semisquare (friction) Neptune and Mercury in the twelfth house. The stimulation signified by the major and minor progressed Mars coincided with the divorce.

The examples provided by these two horoscopes should demonstrate quite clearly the importance of judging the natal chart and its progressions. If they are calculated ahead of time (before the aspects come within the one-degree orb) counseling for these energy-releases can often cause the native to change his life in order to sidestep sorrow and tragedy.

However, for the study at hand, the most important concept to remember is the influence mapped in the contestant's own chart. It forms the backdrop to an intelligent appraisal of all situations.

(1) How to Read Cosmodynes, AFA Tempe, AZ
(2) The Church of Light, Los Angeles, CA
(3) American Federation of Astrologers, Tempe, AZ

9. AUXILIARY AIDS

There are several other supplementary factors related to contest charts which we should be aware off. They are not as important or hold as much weight as the foregoing techniques. But they can be used to enhance the native's power and luck to attract a win.

By choosing a best time to enter a contest (if the time element allows freedom of choice), the contestant can take advantage of the supportive energies mapped by progressed aspects as described in the last chapter. Remember that this progressed aspect lasts for a span of time as it is operative while one degree applying and one degree separating the partile or exact aspect.

Sometime during that period two ephemeral techniques can be considered to choose a day that will strengthen the contestant's chances of winning. they involve a specific transiting Moon aspect and/or a specific planetary hour activity when action should be initiated.

MOON ASPECT

Everyday affairs, the common people, general trends come under the Moon's rule. Thus, if a period before the contest allows it, select a day in the ephemeris when transiting Moon forms a harmonious aspect with the planet, Midheaven or Ascendant which the cosmodyne report lists as having not only power (attraction) but also a certain amount of harmony (luck). By expending the energy on that day, the basic harmony within the native is energized into activity and coincides with a boost in attractive power.

Look at Jenner's Cosmodyne Report in Chapter 8. The most powerful points in his chart are the Sun, the Ascendant, the Midheaven and the Moon. However, they all appear in the discord column, showing a certain amount of restriction. If they are emphasized, they would represent little or no help. In fact, obstacles could be encouraged. Pluto is next in power with 8% of the chart energy, while at the same time being listed as tops in harmony at 31.5%, indicating supportive energy.

When looking in the ephemeris to select that special day to enter the contest, Jenner should do so on a day when the transiting Moon and transiting Pluto form a harmonious aspect with each other in the sky. (Again, this depends upon whether that date allows the right time element.) If no such aspect can be found within the time span of the active progression(s), then not to worry. As long as the stimulation appears in the natal chart and its progressions, he will have support for the venture.

PLANETARY HOURS

Sometimes such a favorable Moon aspect is not available (or even if it is), there is another moderate stimulation that might be added. A planetary hour ruled by Pluto (Jenner's most harmonious planet) can be chosen to launch the project. But, remember that these planetary hours are less significant. Having the progressions to show and support action is stronger evidence for winning than mere planetary hours.

Going back to basics when we cast a horoscope, we note that the Midheaven remains at the same sign, degree and minute of the zodiac for all latitudes. However, this is not true of the Ascendant, which varies for every locality (due to the bulge of the globe).

That means that the Ascendant degree and minute changes with varying latitudes. In fact, every four minutes a different degree of the zodiac rises over the Ascendant and falls over the Descendant.

Because sunrise is represented by the Ascendant (first house cusp) and sunset by the Descendant (seventh house cusp) the hours for sunrise and sunset change not only due to latitude but day to day during the different seasons of the year. Most daily newspapers list the time of sunrise and sunset at the place of publication, so it is easy enough to check this phenomena.

Hours of sunrise and sunset are the perimeters of finding planetary hours -- day hours or night hours. There are planetary hour tables in magazines and textbooks. Often they need to be interpolated for precise latitudes (including the minutes). However, these hours are easy enough to calculate from scratch yourself.

To find a day hour, first calculate the span of hours, minutes and seconds from sunrise to sunset. Then divide this time interval by twelve to find the length of a planetary hour on that day. The time interval from sunset to sunrise divided by twelve yields the length of the night planetary hour. As you can see, planetary hours are not of the same duration as clock hours. Each planetary hour is one-twelfth of its time span -- day or night.

The first planetary hour after sunrise is ruled by the planet representing that day: Sunday, the Sun; Monday, the Moon; Tuesday, Mars; Wednesday, Mercury; Thursday, Jupiter; Friday, Venus; and Saturday, Saturn.

This sequence is followed, each in order, over and over again. The higher octave planets occupy the same position in the sequence as their lower octave expressions. The Moon is the lower octave of Pluto; Venus is the lower octave of Neptune; and Mercury is the lower octave of Uranus. The sequence of hours reads Sun, Venus (or Neptune), Mercury (or Uranus), Moon (or Pluto), Saturn, Jupiter, Mars, Sun, Venus, etc., all through the hours of day and night.

Take Jenner's chart. That Moon-Pluto aspect we spoke of above occurred, say, on a Wednesday. The Pluto hour on that day would be the second planetary hour, because Mercury always represents the first planetary hour on a Wednesday, and Pluto (or the Moon) comes after Mercury (or Uranus) in the sequence of planetary rulers.

Thus, to emphasize the harmony signified by Pluto, we would find the time interval between sunrise and sunset on that date, divide by twelve, then find the second planetary hour after the hour of sunrise on that day. That planetary hour would be the best time for Jenner to take action.

To clarify the procedure we will take an example and work it out, using an even-degree latitude to make the calculation simpler. Our problem: What is the fourth planetary hour ruler on December 30, 1984 at latitude 40N00?

I consulted Raphael's 1984 Ephemeris[1] for the following basic information. On this date sunrise occurred at 7:22 a.m., and the sunset at 4:44 p.m. The time span between these two clock times is seven hours and twenty-two minutes. This represents 442 minutes.

We divide 442 by 12 to find the length of a planetary hour on that day. It is 36 minutes and 10 seconds. The amount is small because on December 30, 1984 in northern latitudes we had just passed the shortest day of the year. Three times the 36 minutes and 10 seconds will give us the clock time of day representing the beginning of the fourth planetary hour on that day. It is a Monday, so the first hour will be ruled by the Moon. 3 X 36" 10' equals 1 hr 48 m 10 s. Sunrise is at 7:22 a.m.+ 1:48:10 (length of 3 planetary hours)9:10:10 a.m. (the start of the fourth planetary hour)on December 30, 1984 at latitude 40N00

What planet rules the fourth planetary hour on that day? As the day is a Monday, the Moon rules the first hour; the second, by Mars; the third, by Mercury; and the fourth, by Jupiter (see sequence listing above).

ELECTIONAL CHART

Another approach is based upon the actual start of a contest. A chart cast for that moment is called an electional chart, set for the date, place, and moment the contest begins. There are several reasons why this approach does not always provide enlightening information. For instance, races of short duration, such as the four minute mile (or less), downhill skiing, swimming heats, and such sometimes consume only a few minutes and seconds. Recall that it takes approximately four minutes for the Ascendant of a chart to shift one degree in the zodiac.

Then there is the accurate start time. Even though times for contests are posted, they do not always begin at that exact minute. If a start is delayed, the chart positions will be affected.

However, if an electional chart is cast for the actual start of a contest, such as a prize fight, the chart can be rotated up over the Ascendant to gain information. C.C. Zain describes this technique clearly in his Horary Astrology: [2]

"In a contest of short duration, such as an athletic contest, the turning points in the contest and the direction they take, are often shown by planets carried by the diurnal rotation of the earth to the conjunction of the first, seventh, tenth and fourth house cusps. A planet having more degrees in the zodiac than such cusp, is carried to the conjunction of the cusp at the rate of about four minutes for each degree removed from the cusp. Thus, if the tenth cusp shows one degree, and Saturn is in Virgo 16 degrees, in a prize fight, if it lasted sixty minutes the challenger at that time would probably be knocked out.

"When, during a conflict, a malefic crosses the cusp of the first or the tenth, the challenger, home team, or first party, is apt to have a difficult time; but if the malefic crosses the cusp of the seventh or the fourth the champion, visiting team, or second party, suffers reverses. But when a benefic crosses the cusp of the first or tenth house, the tide of luck turns in favor of the challenger, home team, or first party; and when a benefic crosses the cusp of the seventh or fourth, the element of luck is in favor of the champion, visiting team, or second party. When such aspects form often marks the victory of the one and the defeat of the other of the contending forces."

(1) W. Foulsham & Co., Ltd., England
(2) The Church of Light, Los Angeles, CA